WILDFLOWERS
GRASSES & Other Plants
of the
NORTHERN PLAINS and BLACK HILLS

Theodore Van Bruggen
Biology Department
University of South Dakota

4th Edition: 1992
Library of Congress Catalog Card No.: 83-71125
ISBN No.: 0-912410-05-1 Softcover

Organized in 1959, the Badlands Natural History Association is a
nonprofit corporation dedicated to assisting the National Park
Service in its scientific, educational, historical, and interpretive
activities. It is recognized by the Service as an official cooperating
association operating in Badlands National Park and is
incorporated under the laws of the State of South Dakota.

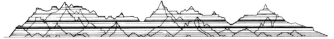

Cover and Design Concept by Christina Watkins
Printed by Fenske Printing Inc., Rapid City, South Dakota

Foreword

The Northern Great Plains and Black Hills are fascinating to many residents and visitors. For those wanting to know more about this unique region, a knowledge of the grasses and flowers significant to the area is an invaluable place to start. It is particularly fitting that the Badlands Natural History Association has published this book in its 33rd year of operation, and that Dr. Theodore Van Bruggen has accepted the task of developing his fourth revised edition.

Dr. Van Bruggen, a professor at the University of South Dakota, is a renowned plant taxonomist and biologist as well as a recognized authority on the flora of the Northern Plains and Black Hills. He authored a manual of the **Vascular Plants of South Dakota** which was published by the Iowa State Press in 1985, and co-authored the **Flora of the Great Plains** in 1986.

Armed with this book, patience and curiosity, the reader can spend many happy hours in the field and at home learning about this vital part of America.

Irv Mortenson
Superintendent, Badlands National Park

Acknowledgments

For a number of years, I have had an interest in the flora of South Dakota, and have had a hobby of photographing plants which are used in plant systematics classes at the University of South Dakota. In 1967, Mr. John Stockert, then an Interpretive Naturalist at the Badlands National Monument, encouraged me to work on a first edition, published in 1970. His expertise and guidance are still gratefully acknowledged in this fourth edition.

If you are interested in hunting for wildflowers, you may not have to go any further than the right-of-way of a nearby road or railway. To experience a large expanse of native prairie, more effort may be necessary, as there are only a few such areas remaining. The land can adjust on its own quite delicately to the vagaries of the climate, but man's presence has brought a new element which is sometimes felt in the harshest of terms. Eroded gullies, past dust storms, overgrazing, and abandoned farmsteads attest to man's unwillingness or inability to live within the laws of nature. Extensive cultivation, draining potholes, cutting timber, and other acts of man have made many native plants of the high plains extremely rare.

I appreciate the use of the poem by Dr. Norman H. Russell which expresses very well my sentiments of joy in studying plants.

To Mrs. Myrtle Kravig of Lead, South Dakota; Mr. George Kellogg of Rapid City, South Dakota; and Mr. Stockert, I am indebted for their special interest and generosity in supplying a portion of the photographs.

Finally, I wish to give recognition to my wife, Gerry, who has accompanied me on **many** collecting trips in the region. Her patience, interest and help are much appreciated.

Theodore Van Bruggen

TURKS-CAP LILY   *Lilium canadense*
1/3x Van Bruggen photo   See inside front cover.

SMALL SOAPWEED
1/5x Stockert photo

Yucca glauca
See inside front cover.

Introduction

By a conservative estimate, there are about 2,000 species of flowering plants native to the northern plains and Black Hills of the United States. Of these species, 312 have been chosen as characteristic representatives for this book. This region, roughly 600 miles square, includes the western parts of Minnesota and Iowa, all of North Dakota and South Dakota and Nebraska, and the eastern parts of Montana and Wyoming. The area lies within the large geographic sector known as the Grassland Province, which extends as a broad, north-south belt through mid-continent from Alberta to Texas. It has a climate of hot, semi-humid to dry summers and cold winters.

Variations in temperature and rainfall profoundly affect the establishment and distribution of plants and animals. In extreme situations, temperatures in the northern plains and Black Hills vary from 116 degrees to more than 40 degrees below zero Fahrenheit! The average yearly precipitation ranges from about 14 inches in the western plains to nearly 29 inches in the eastern part; the northern Black Hills may receive about 30 inches. In the plains, more than one-half of this precipitation falls just before and during the growing season.

As rainfall increases from the Rockies eastward, the vegetation of the Great Plains changes from shortgrass prairie in the west, to mixedgrass prairie through the middle, and to tallgrass prairies in the east. Occasional stands of native, deciduous forests occur in the eastern part of the grassland, and further east the tallgrass prairie ultimately gives way to deciduous forests. Because of extensive cultivation, the interlacing of prairie and forest along the eastern edge of the grassland is hard to see. Only in protected areas, such as in some ravines and along stream courses, are vestiges of native forests found.

The Black Hills of South Dakota and Wyoming form a striking contrast within the Grassland Province. The mountainous habitat, with its greater precipitation, supports many species not found in the surrounding prairie. Almost one-fourth of these Black Hills species are also widespread in the Rocky Mountains which are more than 300 miles west.

The preparation of this fourth edition incorporates a response to many requests received to enlarge the volume, including other typical plants of the prairie. For the first section of the book, I've chosen well-known grasses, sedges, rushes, and other plants which do not have showy flowers, but nonetheless are dominant plants of the prairie. The incorporation of these less-showy plants also fulfills requests of those who use this volume with technical manuals in the identification of plants. I hope that students of all ages and professionals, such as biology teachers, outdoor educators, conservationists and applied biologists in general, will utilize this book to become better acquainted with their natural surroundings.

For easy identification, the second through the fifth sections in this volume are grouped according to color, with the yellows first, then the whites, reds, and blues. In some instances, particularly between the red and blue sections, it was difficult to place certain species which vary widely in color or which may appear to some individuals to be more like one color but to others more like another. If there is question as to which section a flower belongs, please check more than one section. Within each of the four color groups, the arrangement is according to blooming season with those flowering earliest shown first.

Among other things, the descriptions for each plant include the approximate blooming dates, general habitat, type of plant, and an x-factor. Flowering dates vary, depending on the terrain slope, moisture availability, the elevation of the plant if in the Black Hills, and, to a lesser degree, the latitude and exposure of the site where the plant grows. The captions also include, if known, some pioneer and Indian uses. An x-factor is shown under each description to indicate how much smaller or larger the illustration is compared to the actual flower.

Fortunately, some tracts of native prairie have purposely been protected and preserved. These areas, though some are not large, include Agate Fossil Beds

National Monument, Nebraska; Badlands National Park, South Dakota; Cayler Prairie near Lake Park in northwest Iowa; Little Bighorn National Monument Montana; Pipestone National Monument, Minnesota; Siesche Hollow State Park near Sisseton, South Dakota; and Theodore Roosevelt National Park, North Dakota.

In recent years, the Nature Conservancy has acquired several large tracts of prairie for permanent preservation, as well as a number of smaller tracts in the Northern Plains states. Two are worthy of mention: the Ordway Memorial Prairie, located in northern South Dakota, approximately 7,600 acres in size; and the Niobrara Valley Preserve, in north central Nebraska, over 50,000 acres, are striking expanses of native prairie in our region.

There is not a **best** time to see the prairie. Late spring and late summer, perhaps, bring the more showy displays of wild flowers, but any time is a good time to visit. The ways in which seeds and spores are distributed, how rain and snow are held in the topsoil, and how the gradual decay of plant and animal remains enrich the land can all be noticed when the prairie is not in bloom.

Native plants should never be wantonly collected or destroyed. Many are transplanted with success, but certain species—and they usually are rare—need environmental conditions that are difficult or impossible to duplicate in gardens or lawns. Orchids, lilies, gentians, and evening-primroses are among many in this category. On the other hand, many asters, penstemons, and cacti grow easily when transplanted.

Here is a suggestion. Do what many who are sensitive to the preciousness of our prairies and forests have done. Go **hunting** with a camera! Many excellent, inexpensive, single-lens-reflex cameras are available. With a little practice and patience, a trip to the prairie will be highly rewarding and may be relived many times.

GIANT BUR-REED

Sparganium eurycarpum Bur-reed Family
June - September

Bur-reeds are usually found rooted in the mud
or shallow water in wet meadows, marshes, or
other wet places across the United States. The
stems are erect, up to 3 feet or more tall, and
they have an extensive rhizome system that
makes them perennial. Their leaves are strap-like
and ascending. The outstanding feature of Giant
Bur-reed is the inflorescence or flower cluster. It
is branched and erect with male and female
flowers in separate globose clusters, the male
above and white, the female greenish and below.
The fruits that mature from the greenish pistils
are called achenes, hardened nut-like structures
that serve as food for wildlife.

1/2x Van Bruggen photo

Ferns, Grasses and Grassy-Like Plants

NARROW-LEAVED CAT-TAIL

Typha angustifolia Cat-tail Family July - August
This cat-tail has leaves less than ½ inch wide on slender, 3 to 7 foot
tall stems. When the flowering spikes appear, the male flowers
above are separated by a short interval of the stem from the female
flowers below. After flowering, the male flowers, consisting only of
pollen-producing stamens and sterile hairs, drop from the flowering spike. The female spikes mature many small, hairy seeds that
break free in the wind. Indian tribes used the downy material to
line diapers for their babies as well as to stuff it into sacks for
mattresses.

1/5x Van Bruggen photo

BROAD-LEAVED CAT-TAIL

Typha latifolia Cat-tail Family July - August
This photograph shows a more mature condition, after the male
flowers had dropped from the stem. As the common name indicates, this cat-tail has leaves usually over 1 inch wide. The stems
and spikes are more robust than the narrow-leaved cat-tail. The
male flowering spike is above and adjacent to the female spike,
lacking the open interval typical of the narrow-leaved cat-tail. Both
species grow in similar habitats across the United States, and when
near each other, often produce hybrids with some characteristics of
each parent.

1/4x Van Bruggen photo

FOX SEDGE

Carex vulpinoidea Sedge Family June - July

There are nearly one hundred species of the genus **Carex** in the north temperate United States, many occurring in the Great Plains. Appearing as a grass from afar, they have many different inflorescences and flowering structures when viewed with a hand lens or microscope. The fox sedge is a common inhabitant of sloughs and marshes. It is a perennial from stout rootstocks; the stems are about 2 feet tall; and the fruiting cluster has needle-like awns projecting from the bracts, resembling a fox tail, hence the common name. The male and female flowers are separate but adjacent in dense clusters.

2/3x Van Bruggen photo

SAW-BEAK SEDGE

Carex stipata Sedge Family July - August

This is called Saw-beak because of the elongate, serrated beaks surrounding the fruit or achene at maturity when the fruiting spike becomes a tawny brown color. This feature can easily be seen with a hand lens which magnifies to a power of ten. The sedges appear as a formidable group to beginners, but after a little learning, they are fascinating to identify. Common throughout North America, this sedge grows in wet, low places. The stems are sharply triangular, stout, and up to 3 feet tall. In this sedge, the male flowers are formed in small, individual spikes. After pollination they disintegrate, leaving the maturing female fruits shown here.

2/3x Van Bruggen photo

STRICT SEDGE

Carex stricta Sedge Family July - August

This common sedge grows in tussocks or large, elevated clumps in marshes and swamps throughout the temperate United States. The specific and common name comes from the strict or tight, narrow arrangement of male and female spikes at the top of the stems. Note that the male flowers are dark brown to purple, above the green, lower female flowers. This **Carex** is distinguished by the color and arrangement of the dense, overlapping scales in the female flower spikes. The stems may be over 3 feet tall, the lower one-third a dark red, turning brown.

2/3x Van Bruggen photo

SLENDER FLATSEDGE

Cyperus odoratus Sedge Family July - August

This annual sedge is typical of the more than fifteen species of the genus **Cyperus** which grow in the Great Plains. Nearly all grow in moist or wet places. They are characterized by being grassy in appearance; however, their stems are usually triangular in cross section. They also have relatively wide basal leaves and a tuft of leaves immediately below the widely radiating branches of the flowering head. Plants are light green, and grow in clumps from 12 to 18 inches tall. It is best recognized by the two-rowed, spike-like flower clusters which become brown at maturity.

1/3x Van Bruggen photo

RED-STEMMED SPIKESEDGE

Eleocharis erythropoda Sedge Family June - July

Red-stemmed spikesedge is a common inhabitant of all types of moist or marshy places in the Northern Plains. Of small stature, the plant seldom exceeds 1½ feet. It grows in tufts or clumps, forming large mats. The stems are slender and wiry, with pronounced reddish bases and roots, hence the common name. As in other members of the genus **Eleocharis**, its leaves are reduced to sheaths around the stem, with photosynthetic functions carried out by the green stem. The flowering spikelet is solitary at the top of the stem, mostly less than ½ inch long, becoming brown at maturity.

1½x Van Bruggen photo

SPIKE SEDGE

Eleocharis macrostachya Sedge Family June - July

There are about a dozen spike rushes native or naturalized in the Great Plains. Some are annual but some of the most common are perennial, forming dark green mats in moist meadows, edges of ponds, and in marshes. This spike rush grows to 3 feet from an extensive rhizome system. The stems are dark green, mostly without leaves, and topped by a single, cone-like group of flowers called a spikelet. Within the overlapping scales of the spikelet the small, lenticular or lens-shaped achenes develop. The spikelet is usually ½ inch in length, becoming brown at maturity. Often the upper part of the stem is flattened. This spike rush is tolerant of brackish and alkaline conditions, so is widespread in the Plains.

1x Van Bruggen photo

RIVER BULRUSH

Scirpus fluviatilis Sedge Family June - August

River bulrush is distinct from the other bulrushes by its stout, sharply triangular stems and dense foliage. The stems are 3 to 6 feet tall, arising from thick, spreading rhizomes. Leaves are ½ to ¾ of an inch wide, well distributed along the stem. The flowering cluster has 10 to 30 or more cone-like spikelets at the top of the stem, some sessile, others branched in a very irregular fashion. Each of the spikelets is an inch or more long and becomes a tan color in early autumn. Forming large stands in shallow backwaters, oxbows of rivers, as well as in marshes or potholes, this sedge is tolerant of alkali. It is widespread over the United States.

1/2x Van Bruggen photo

SOFT-STEM BULRUSH

Scirpus validus Sedge Family June - August

Perhaps our best known and common bulrush, this also has the common name of tule. The light green stems are soft and cylindrical, with inner spongy tissue that is easily crushed between thumb and finger. Soft-stem often grows to 6 or more feet tall. A perennial from knotty rhizomes, it has leaves that are near the base of the stem, mostly reduced to membranous sheaths around the stem. The inflorescence or flower cluster is open and branched, with many spikelets or clusters, each about ½ inch long, becoming brown at maturity. The fruits or achenes are eaten by waterfowl. This bulrush is common throughout North America in all types of marshy or aquatic habitats.

2/3x Van Bruggen photo

DARK GREEN BULRUSH

Scirpus atrovirens Sedge Family June - August

This bulrush is found in marshy areas and wet meadows throughout the Plains. It is recognized by the narrow stems 3 to 5 feet tall, the well-developed leaves up to ½ inch wide or more, and by the irregularly-branched flower clusters that are globose or roughly spherical in shape. Another feature that distinguishes this bulrush are the long, spreading leaf-like bracts at the base of the flower cluster, making the latter appear terminal or at the top of the stem. Like most of the bulrushes, this one is perennial but has short fibrous roots, lacking the long, stout rhizomes common in others.

1/3x Van Bruggen photo

CHAIR-MAKER'S RUSH

Scirpus pungens Sedge Family July - September

This bulrush is also known by the name three-square because of the sharp, triangular cross section of the stem. Growing to 3 feet or more, the stems are stout and wiry, with 3 to 5 short, ascending basal leaves. A perennial, it spreads by reddish rhizomes in fresh to brackish or alkaline marshes, particularly in sandy areas. Widespread in the United States, Chair-maker's Rush can be found over the Great Plains. The flowering clusters or spikelets are sessile, from 1 to 5 in number, and appear to be lateral near the top of the green, triangular stem. Each spikelet is about ½ inch long, cone-like, with many overlapping scales in which the small fruits, called achenes, develop in late summer.

1x Van Bruggen photo

TORREY'S RUSH

Juncus torreyi Rush Family July - September

Of the nearly two dozen species of true rushes native or naturalized in the Great Plains, this is perhaps the most common representative. A marsh or shallow water inhabitant, this rush is a perennial with rounded, grass-like green stems. Forming large clumps, single stems arise from spreading rhizomes that have tuberous thickenings. The leaves are few and reduced in size, erect and long-tapering. The flowers form in 3 to 6 globose clusters at the top of the stem. They are green and not very conspicuous until late in the season when they become a rich, tawny brown as shown here.

1/3x Van Bruggen photo

REED CANARYGRASS

Phalaris arundinacea Grass Family June - July

Although a native of North America, much of the Reed Canarygrass now growing in temperate America has become naturalized from seed sources in Northern Europe. This grass is a coarse, cool season plant whose stems grow to 7 feet tall in moist, fertile soil areas. It has a very dense underground system of roots and rhizomes. Having a light green color with waxy or glaucous bloom, it is somewhat inconspicuous in early summer when it makes most of its growth. Later, however, its seed head, a contracted panicle, matures to a golden yellow color. Then this grass becomes noticeable, the reason why the accompanying photograph was chosen. Reed Canarygrass is planted as pasture mixture, in waterways, and for hay or grazing.

1/3x Van Bruggen photo

JUNEGRASS

Koeleria pyramidata Grass Family June - July

Junegrass is common throughout the Great Plains in upland prairies, sandhills and open woods. A tufted perennial reaching 2 feet, the narrow stems are slender with most leaves arising from the base of the plant. The inflorescence or flower cluster is contracted and almost spike-like, silvery-green, 3 to 5 inches long. After the seeds are set, the entire plant becomes a golden yellow, when it is most noticeable. A good forage grass, Junegrass almost always occurs in scattered stands.

1/4x Van Bruggen photo

SQUIRRELTAIL

Sitanion hystrix Grass Family June - July

Squirreltail grows as a loose to densely tufted perennial in dry or clayey soils from the eastern Dakotas westward to British Columbia. It is easily recognized by the many very stiff, needle-like lateral awns in the flowering spike. These awns may be 3 inches long. Late in the season they are very raspy and may cause eye and mouth injury to grazing animals. Several stems arise from the crown of each plant and reach 1 to 1½ feet tall. Often the stems and leaves may have a reddish or purplish cast. Squirreltail is of interest to botanists because it hybridizes with the wild ryes and wheatgrasses.

1/3x Van Bruggen photo

REDTOP

Agrostis stolonifera Grass Family June - August

As the species name indicates, this perennial grass has stolons or runners above or below the soil surface. It is not uncommon for a single plant to spread to a diameter of 3 feet. The common name refers to the reddish cast the pyramidal seed head possesses during much of its development. The culms, or stems, are often 2 feet or more tall and very leafy. Redtop is found in much of the Great Plains, ranging from the east to west coast. It can tolerate wet or dry conditions, acid or alkaline soils. Several varieties are planted to pasture and used on golf courses.

1/4x Van Bruggen photo

WESTERN WHEATGRASS

Agropyron smithii Grass Family June - August

There are more than a dozen Wheatgrasses native to the Great Plains of North America. This species is perhaps best known. Reaching 2 feet or more in height, this grass is easily recognized by its blue, waxy appearance. The flower spike is composed of 10-25 stiff, erect clusters of spikelets. These are alternately arranged at the summit of the leafy stem. Each of the spikelets have 6 to 10 flowers, a characteristic which differentiates it from the other wheatgrasses. It is a good soil binder with maximum growth in early spring. Very nutritious, it can withstand heavy grazing. In many states this grass is planted in highway right-of-ways.

1/3x Van Bruggen photo

GREEN NEEDLEGRASS

Stipa viridula Grass Family June - July

Green needlegrass is a tufted perennial with narrowly leaved, slender stems 2 to 3 feet tall. It is a native, growing in upland prairie throughout the Great Plains, reaching farther west in its distribution than Porcupine grass. The flowering and fruiting head is narrowly branched. The awns, only about 1 inch long, radiate out from the central axis of the head. Late in the season the green inflorescence turns gray-green and then a pale straw color. A cool season perennial, green needlegrass is valuable for forage in early spring and again in the fall.

1/5x Van Bruggen photo

PORCUPINE GRASS

Stipa spartea Grass Family July - August

There are over two dozen needle-grasses, members of the **Stipa** genus, that are native to North America. In our area of the Great Plains, this grass is well known. A cool season bunch grass, the stems reach 2 to 4 feet tall in early summer. At this time it is good forage grass. It becomes conspicuous when the large, drooping heads produce the mature seeds with their long, twisted awns. These may be 6 or more inches long. Very pointed when mature, these seeds are injurious to livestock. After the seeds drop, the two yellow, erect glumes or bracts remain at the top of the stems. A close relative, needle-and-thread, is often confused with this grass. It has a shorter seed husk, or lemma, to which the awn is attached.

1/4x Van Bruggen photo

LITTLE BLUESTEM

Andropogon scoparius Grass Family July - September

Little Bluestem is not very noticeable in the prairie until late summer or early fall. After a frost the vegetative parts become a warm bronze color. The seed heads are on solitary branches and, when mature, are densely hairy. The stems are usually 1 to 2½ feet tall, growing from a tufted base that may have short rhizomes. This common upland prairie native ranges from the east coast to the Rockies in the west, reaching its greatest abundance in the southern plains of Kansas and Oklahoma. It is a nutritious forage grass and makes good winter hay.

1/3x Van Bruggen photo

BIG BLUESTEM

Andropogon gerardi Grass Family August - October

Of the seventeen or so species of *Andropogon* native to the United States, the best known is Big Bluestem. It is a major component of the Tallgrass prairie in the eastern Great Plains. Perhaps no other grass is as important in terms of forage value for livestock. It grows from bottom lands to uplands. Commonly reaching 6 feet or more in height, this grass is conspicuous by its "turkey-foot" branching of the seed head. Its stems have a bluish to bronze cast in late summer, hence the common name. Big Bluestem is a warm season grass with short, scaly rhizomes. It has a dense, tufty growth above and below the roots which may occupy almost all of the upper 1 to 2 feet of soil space. This grass is truly the "prince of the prairie."

1/3x Van Bruggen photo

SAND BLUESTEM

Andropogon hallii Grass Family August - October

Sand bluestem is conspicuous in late summer and early fall in the western one-half of the Great Plains by virtue of its hairy white seed heads. The stems are stout, 3 to 7 feet tall, and wave like flags in the prairie. As the common name implies, it is particularly adapted to sandy soils, and in much of its range is called sandhills bluestem. It forms dense colonies because of its creeping, scaly rhizomes. In areas of less than 30 inches of average annual rainfall this grass dominates, whereas big bluestem does best with more than this average amount. Typical of the bluestems, it is a valuable forage grass of the plains.

1/4x Van Bruggen photo

HAIRY GRAMA

Bouteloua hirsuta Grass Family July - August

Hairy Grama is more southern in its distribution in the Plains than the other grama grasses, rarely occurring as far north as North Dakota. A perennial bunchgrass, its stems may reach 15 inches. True to its common name, the leaf sheaths and seed heads are hairy. This characteristic, along with the projected needle-like point of the seed spikes, clearly distinguishes it from blue grama. Hairy grama is rarely found in solid stands. It grows in a variety of rocky to shallow, sandy soil, and withstands extreme drought. Its foliage cures naturally in the fall, turning pale green and then light brown. It is a valuable late fall and winter range plant for livestock.

1/2x Van Bruggen photo

BLUE GRAMA

Bouteloua gracilis Grass Family July - September

Blue Grama is a most important range grass of the Great Plains. Its curly, narrow leaves, 3 to 6 inches long, only narrowly overtopped by the seed stems, make it appear very similar to Hairy Grama. Blue Grama has one-sided seed spikes like teeth on a comb that curve upon reaching maturity. They are not as hairy and lack the needle-like points beyond the spike. It is densely tufted, often with short rhizomes, and forms thick mats which aid in building soil and preventing erosion. This grass withstands drought very well and during dry periods provides a major part of the diet of range animals.

1x Van Bruggen photo

SIDE-OATS GRAMA

Bouteloua curtipendula Grass Family July - September

Side-oats is widely distributed, not only in the Great Plains, but from Maine to southern California. Like the other grama grasses, it has its oat-like "seeds" that hang downward in two rows in the stem axis. This is the basis for its common name. It grows in a variety of upland soils. The stems or culms are from 1 to almost 3 feet tall. A perennial, it has scaly underground rhizomes beginning growth in early April. A cool season grass, during the hot summer the leaves curl and become a whitish brown. By this time the seeds are beginning to mature. During early fall it has another period of growth, making it a valuable forage grass for all livestock.

1/3x Van Bruggen photo

BLUE JOINT

Calamagrostis canadensis Grass Family July - August

Blue Joint grass is one of several reedgrasses found in the temperate parts of North America. It grows in marshes and swales of prairies or in open woods near streams or lakes. The stems are 3 to 5 feet tall, growing from strong, creeping rhizomes. The inflorescence, or seed head, is a branched panicle. It may vary from being narrow and contracted or wide and expanded. Early in the summer it is green, but becomes this characteristic tawny brown in late summer, when it is easily recognized. The stems are erect and leafy, persisting until late fall. It is a good forage grass before it reaches maturity. Then it becomes tough and unpalatable to livestock.

1/3x Van Bruggen photo

CANADA WILD RYE

Elymus canadensis Grass Family July - August

Of the nearly two dozen Wild Rye grasses in the United States, this is the best known representative. A dominant grass of our prairies, it ranges from coast to coast in open soil of all types. Reaching 2 to 4 feet in height, it is recognized by the green, waxy color of the pointed leaves and later by its nodding flowering spikes with long, curved awns. A perennial bunchgrass, it resumes growth early in spring and again in the fall after the seed spikes have matured. Because of its cool season growth habit, it is desirable for spring and fall pasturing. Many strains of Canada Wild Rye have been developed and planted, principally to revegetate range and prairie areas after overgrazing and erosion.

1/2x Van Bruggen photo

COMMON REED

Phragmites australis Grass Family July - September

Common Reed is perhaps the tallest of our grasses, reaching 8 feet tall. It grows in marshes or in water of streams or at the edges of lakes. The word **Phragmites** comes from the Greek, meaning "growing like a hedge or fence along streams." Stems of common reed are stout, bolting up every few inches from spreading rhizomes or stolons. Because of this, the plants are usually found in large colonies. Leaves are flat, up to 1½ inches wide. The flowering cluster is large and terminal, becoming plumose due to the many long, silky hairs in the flowering spikelets. This grass is found throughout the temperate part of the United States. Although not important as a forage grass, its majestic appearance makes it noteworthy.

1/5x Van Bruggen photo

THREE-AWN

Aristida longiseta Grass Family July - August

A variety of common names have been applied to this perennial bunch grass. Not all are very complimentary. Dogtown, wiregrass, and three-awn ticklegrass are but a few. Some of the three-awn grasses are annual. They occur on poor, thin or sandy soils throughout the Plains. They also are one of the first invaders of eroded or overgrazed rangeland. A relatively short grass, it is easily recognized by the three prominent, diverging awns 3 to 4 inches long that are attached at the top of the seed or fruit. Often these awns are red or purple. In other species the awns are of various shorter lengths. This grass is unpalatable and, in general, quite undesireable to the rancher.

1/3x Van Bruggen photo

BUFFALO-GRASS

Buchloe dactyloides Grass Family July - September

Buffalo-grass is a dominant of the short grass prairie of the western Plains. Very drought resistant, it forms a dense, gray-green sod where stems and leaves seldom exceed 5 inches. Buffalo-grass in unique because it is usually dioecious, meaning male plants grow separately from female plants. The male plant is taller, with one-sided spikes which produce the pollen. The female plant is shorter, producing its flowers and 1 to 4 seeds in bur-like heads mostly concealed in the foliage near the soil surface. This grass reproduces by short, vigorous runners which root every 1 to 2 inches. It is an excellent ground cover for erosion control and can be grazed to a limited extent.

1½x Van Bruggen photo

MARSH MUHLY

Muhlenbergia racemosa Grass Family July - September

There are at least fifteen Muhly grasses that grow in the Great Plains area. This one is perhaps as common as the Plains Muhly, *M. cuspidata*, which grows in drier habitats in the Plains. As the common name implies, this perennial grows in marshy areas, meadows and alluvial soils along streams. It has creeping, scaly rhizomes and stems that are stiff and branched at midlength, up to 2 feet or more tall. As in most Muhly grasses, the seed head is a narrow, spike-like panicle with ascending branches. Although not an important forage grass, it is eaten by livestock. The name *Muhlenbergia* commemorates the German-born Lutheran minister Henry Muhlenberg, a pioneer botanist of Pennsylvania in the late 1700's, who was a great student of grasses and sedges.

1/3x Van Bruggen photo

PRAIRIE CORDGRASS

Spartina pectinata Grass Family July - September

Prairie cordgrass or sloughgrass, as it is often called, is one of the most common grasses of low, wet soils in the temperate part of the United States. Forming a heavy, almost woody sod which effectively protects lowland soil from erosion, it can be cut several times in the summer for winter hay. The stems are usually taller than 6 feet, with coarse blades that have sharp teeth on their margins. The seed heads are arranged in branches called panicles. Each branch of the panicle is a spike, and is composed of individual flower clusters called spikelets. These spikelets are arranged in two rows on one side of the spike like teeth on a comb.

1/2x Van Bruggen photo

SWITCHGRASS

Panicum virgatum Grass Family July - September

Switchgrass is a dominant in the tallgrass prairie, occurring throughout the Great Plains. A warm season grass, it is almost as well known to the rancher as big bluestem. It grows in large bunches, vigorously spreading by its many creeping rhizomes. Switchgrass is recognized by its large, panicled seed head, often exceeding 18 inches and almost as wide. The seeds are produced at the ends of the many branches. The leafy stems are usually 2 to 4 feet tall. It prefers the lower, more moist parts of the prairie, but will do well in drier places. It, along with other tall grasses of the prairie, is often cut for winter hay.

1/4x Van Bruggen photo

PRAIRIE SANDREED

Calamovilfa longifolia Grass Family July - September

This imposing, erect grass is tough and wiry, reaching 4 to 6 feet on dry or sandy slopes. The stems and leaves are pale green, later becoming a straw yellow color. A valuable sand or soil binder, its creeping, scaly rhizomes are robust. The flowering panicle is much branched, from 6 to 12 inches long. A warm season grass, it does very well in dry climates. Only palatable in early spring before it becomes tough and wiry, its greatest virtue is to stabilize blow-out areas of sandy soil. Prairie Sandreed is found throughout the Great Plains.

1/3x Van Bruggen photo

INDIANGRASS

Sorghastrum avenaceum Grass Family August - September

Indiangrass is one of the ten or so native species making up the dominant grasses of the midwestern tallgrass prairie. It is infrequent to rare, however, in the far western plains where the shorter grasses dominate. This grass grows to 6 or more feet; the stems are slender, with narrow, ascending leaves. In late summer Indiangrass develops a golden, plume-like flowering head or inflorescence. The arrangement of the hairs and long, twisted awns in the narrowly branched head is distinctive. A warm season grass with short, scaly rhizomes, it forms large patches of sod. Very nutritious, it serves as excellent winter range or prairie hay for winter feeding.

1/4x Van Bruggen photo

RICE CUTGRASS

Leersia oryzoides Grass Family August - September

Rice cutgrass is a common inhabitant of marshes, backwaters of rivers and pond margins. A member of the rice tribe of grasses, the seeds of this grass provide food for migratory waterfowl. This may be the reason for its wide distribution in the United States. A perennial with many rhizomes, Rice cutgrass has weak stems that sprawl but may be more than 3 feet long. It forms a twisted dense growth in large patches in and near the water's edge. This grass is perhaps best known for the razor-sharp leaf margins that can scratch skin severely, even through normal clothing of the legs. The seed head is a branched panicle with small, flat, one-flowered spikelets or flower clusters.

1/3x Van Bruggen photo

PRAIRIE DROPSEED

Sporobolus asper Grass Family August - September

A warm season perennial, prairie dropseed is a bunch grass that is very drought resistant. It grows in dry upland and sandy areas throughout the Plains. This grass has stems 2 to 3 feet tall and is very asymmetrical in its growth. Several characteristics help to identify it. The seed head is 3 to 10 inches long, narrow and almost hidden in the upper leaf sheath. The individual flower clusters or spikelets are very short and each produce one small seed that drops from the maturing head, hence the common name. A common close relative, Sand dropseed, also occurs in the Plains. It is differentiated from prairie dropseed by the prominent tuft of white hairs at the juncture of the leaf blade and the stem.

2/3x Van Bruggen photo

MARE'S TAIL

Hippuris vulgaris Mare's-Tail Family June - July

The scientific name **Hippuris** comes from the Greek meaning horse and tail. Mare's-tail grows in potholes and roadside ditches that have water throughout most of the growing season. A perennial, the dark green stems are not branched and grow to 12 inches from an underground network of rhizomes. Their leaves are in tight circles (whorls) around the stem. Flowers, small and inconspicuous, are produced in axils of upper leaves. They do not have showy petals or sepals. Mare's tail is found sporadically in the northern part of the Plains and into the boreal part of the Northern Hemisphere.

2/3x Van Bruggen photo

GROUND PINE

Lycopodium dendroideum Clubmoss Family June - July

Ground pine is a small, evergreen plant which botanists consider to be very ancient. The stems grow from a perennial underground rhizome, with irregular spreading branches to 12 inches tall. In early summer the upper sessile leaves become compact and fertile, producing small spore-cases called cones or strobili. The small, almost microscopic yellowish spores are released and later germinate to reproduce the species. Ground pine is very rare in moist canyons and openings of woods in the northern hemisphere and has been found in the Black Hills of South Dakota and Wyoming.

1/2x Van Bruggen photo

WESTERN POLYPODY

Polypodium hesperium Polypody Family July - August

Western Polypody is often seen in the crevices of granite in the ravines of the Black Hills. It grows on the shady or north-facing slopes. The green to brown leathery fronds are 6 or more inches long and grow from scaly rhizomes that are perennial in the cracks and crevices of the granite. A true fern, it reproduces by fuzzy, uncovered spore cases called sori on the undersides of the frond blade. A closely related species, called the common polypody, is found on Sioux quartzite in eastern South Dakota and east in North America.

1/3x Van Bruggen photo

OSTRICH FERN

Matteuccia struthiopteris Polypody Family June - August

The graceful sterile leaves or fronds of the Ostrich Fern may grow more than 2 feet tall and form an arching vase-like crown. The stem of this fern is black, creeping and branching underground. The spore-bearing or fertile fronds, when produced, are not as tall as the leaves. They grow in a tight cluster from the base and center of the sterile fronds and turn a tawny brown with black bases. Many spores are released over a long period of time from the sori or spore cases. This interesting fern is found in moist ravine bottoms of the Black Hills and in rich woods at the eastern edge of the Great Plains.

1/5x Van Bruggen photo

GREEN SPLEENWORT

Asplenium viride Polypody Family June - August

Wet, shady crevices in limestone is the usual home for the Green Spleenwort. The fronds are less than 6 inches long with 6 to 12 pairs of leaflets called pinnae. Each pinna is only about one-eighth to one-fourth of an inch across. The underside of most pinnae have several sori, or, spore cases. This fern commonly has many dark brown leaf bases that persist for several years in the cluster which contrasts with the green fronds. Green spleenwort is found across the northern parts of the U.S. and Canada, including the Black Hills.

1/2x Van Bruggen photo

MARSH FERN

Thelypteris palustris Polypody Family June - August

This fern is found in a variety of habitats in the Northern Hemisphere. In our region it is found in marshes and springs at the bases of the Sand Hills of Nebraska and South Dakota. The fronds or blades are 12 to 18 inches long, with slender stipes from black, wide-creeping rhizomes. The leaflets or pinnae are pale green, with brown undersides if they are fertile with sori. The fertile fronds are firm and thick, with the edges of pinnae segments rolled over the underside, partially protecting the spore cases. Freshly broken segments of this fern have a pleasant, fragrant odor.

1/4x Van Bruggen photo

RABBITFOOT GRASS

Polypogon monspeliensis Grass Family June - July

This annual grass, naturalized from Europe, is becoming widely established along waterways, in ditches, along the Missouri River, and other wet, waste places in the Great Plains. It first appears as a branched foxtail but the crowded, elongate awns of the seed head later make it very distinctive. About 10 inches or more tall, the stems are several and usually unequal in length. Later in the season the seed heads, or panicles, become light brown, producing many seeds. There is good evidence to suggest that migratory waterfowl have been instrumental in the spread of this grass since the construction of the main stem dams along the Missouri River.

1/3x Van Bruggen photo

INLAND SALTGRASS

Distichlis spicata Grass Family July - August

A wide-ranging plant in most of the Great Plains, the living cells of this grass have a high osmotic concentration, giving it the adaptation to grow in soils high in salt or in alkali flats. A perennial, Inland Saltgrass grows from stiff, scaly rhizomes. Similar to Buffalo-grass, it is dioecious. The male plants are 6-10 inches tall, with yellowish 2-ranked spikes which produce the pollen. The pistillate or female plants are shorter, with fewer flowers and seeds. Cattle and other livestock will eat Saltgrass early in the grazing season but they prefer other grasses if available.

1/3x Van Bruggen photo

SAND DROPSEED

Sporobolus cryptandrus Grass Family August - September

The word **cryptandrus** means "hidden seed," a good description of this grass. The upper leaf sheath covers or hides a major portion of the panicle or seed until late in the season when the head then elongates and drops its seeds. Another field identification of Sand Dropseed is the prominent beard or tuft of silky hairs at the collar or top of the leaf sheaths. This species is an important forage grass in dry and sandy rangeland throughout the Plains. Plants are perennial, with stems commonly exceeding 2 feet tall. The small, long-lived seeds gives this species ability to rapidly recover from over-grazing or drought.

1/5x Van Bruggen photo

SKUNKBUSH SUMAC

Rhus aromatica Cashew Family April - May

This shrub grows 4 to 6 feet high on hillsides, in ravine breaks, and at the edges of bluffs and buttes in the prairie. The vegetation is ill-smelling, hence the common name. Tiny, yellowish flowers begin blooming in clusters along the small woody branches shortly before the three-lobed, hairy leaves appear. Quarter-inch, red fruits ripen in late June and July. Plains Indians used the branches in basketry and ate the berries. Though closely related to Poison-ivy, this sumac is not poisonous.

4x Stockert photo

Yellow Flowers

MISSOURI GOOSEBERRY

Ribes missouriense Saxifrage Family April - May

Typical of wooded hillsides and ravines, this shrub has numerous, woody stems which grow 4 to 5 feet tall. They are irregular and lax, having needle-sharp spines. The delicate flowers vary from white to yellow and are sometimes tinged with purple. They usually bloom before most leaves come out. Fruits ripen to deep purple from late June into September. Indians relished the gooseberry, eating fruits raw or cooking them with grains and meat.

3/4x Van Bruggen photo

PRAIRIE GOLDENPEA

Thermopsis rhombifolia Legume Family April - May

This perennial herb grows on open banks and eroded slopes to about a foot tall. The showy flowers typify the flower structure of the Legume Family. The upright petal is called the banner, and the two side petals are called wings. The remaining two, lower, fused petals form the keel. The keel contains 10 stamens and the ovary, which forms a small, curved seedpod. Indians burned the nearly dried flowers and confined the smoke to arms or legs that suffered from rheumatism.

1/3x Stockert photo

21

NUTTALL VIOLET

Viola nuttallii Violet Family April - June

The name of this perennial commemorates Thomas Nuttall, a noted botanical explorer of the western plains in the early 1800s. This is one of the few violets of temperate North America with lance-shaped leaves. The short-stemmed plant, less than 6 inches tall, bears yellow flowers with brown or purple lines deep in their throats. The herb is inconspicuous in its preferred habitat of prairie sod. However, as it blooms before other plants gain much growth, its flowers make it more noticeable.

2x Stockert photo

SAGEBRUSH BUTTERCUP

Ranunculus glaberrimus Buttercup Family April - June

The five-petaled, waxy flowers of this meadow perennial typify the some two dozen buttercup species growing in the high plains and Black Hills. Usually found in marshy or moist, wooded places, most have dissected leaves. The fruit resembles a strawberry, with many one-seeded fruits, called achenes, crowded on a receptacle. This herb has a toxic compound that may produce ulcers in grazing animals.

3x Stockert photo

LEAFY MUSINEON

Musineon divaricatum Parsley Family April - June

This native herb of the northern plains was called Wild Parsley by pioneers because of its similarity to the cultivated form. The stem, growing from a thick, perennial root, is short with spreading leaves that are compounded into many segments. The small, yellow flowers are arranged in a tight umbel, an umbrella-like flower cluster with all the flower stalks originating from one point. Each umbel is about 1 inch across. The oval fruits have oil tubes which are characteristic of the Parsley Family. The roots are bitter and probably were not eaten by Indians except in periods of famine.

1x Stockert photo

COMMON DANDELION

Taraxacum officinale Aster Family April - October

The nemesis of a weed-free lawn, Common Dandelion is notorious for growing in places where it is not wanted. A European native, it has invaded most of temperate North America. It is a unique living organism to biologists because it can set seed without pollination or fertilization. This characteristic has developed many forms that differ from each other in small but significant ways. The dandelion is one of the highly evolved members of the plant world. A prolonged warm spell may cause the perennial herb to flower during any "off season" month.

1/2x Van Bruggen photo

GOLDEN CURRANT

Ribes odoratum Saxifrage Family mid April - June

This showy flower with a red center has a spicy odor. Woody stems reach a height of 4 to 10 feet. The lack of spines on these stems distinguishes the currants from the gooseberries which also belong to the genus **Ribes**. The small leaves of Golden Currant are deeply three-lobed. Plants grow principally on rocky hillsides and on north-facing slopes of ravines. The berries which ripen in late June and July make excellent jam and wine. Sioux Indians used the tart, bluish-black currants in making pemmican. The shrub is commonly grown as an ornamental in this region.

1x Stockert photo

WAVYLEAF FALSE-DANDELION

Microseris cuspidata Aster Family late April - May

This herb, also called Prairie Dandelion, has flowers that are quite similar to Common Dandelion (see above), although this one has long, wavy-edged leaves with a whitened line of hairs on each edge. Lacking aboveground stems, the leaves are borne at soil level. The flower heads, slightly broader than those of Common Dandelion, are at the tops of leafless stems called scapes, that are about 10 inches long. Usually the blossoms are open only in the forenoon. This perennial is a native in the north central plains where it tends to grow in patches in moist prairies.

3x Stockert photo

CLEFT GROMWELL

Lithospermum incisum Borage Family late April - June

The yellow flowers of this prairie herb are each about ½ inch long and are almost hidden by leaf-like bracts. The petals have a fringed or crinkled margin. The generic name **Lithospermum**, meaning "stoneseed," refers to the hard, whitened fruits that develop later. Plains Indians used the woody taproot for food and medicine. There is also a purple juice in the roots of this perennial and of a closely related species, Hoary Gromwell (**L. canescens**), which was used as a dye. Cleft Gromwell, also called Puccoon, is frequently found on prairies, especially in the western part of the plains.

1x Stockert photo

LOUISIANA BLADDERPOD

Lesquerella ludoviciana Mustard Family late April - June

Each flower of this perennial has four, regular, yellow petals that form a cross; this is the typical petal arrangement of the Mustard Family. The spherical fruiting pods, almost ¼ inch in diameter, are topped with a short beak. The seeds within were occasionally used for food by prairie Indians. The stems, attaining a height of 12 inches or more, bear leaves that are spatula-shaped, with the widest part towards the tip. Animals generally avoid this herb when grazing. This is but one of a number of bladderpods that inhabit the prairies in dry, sandy areas.

3x Stockert photo

COMMON LOUSEWORT

Pedicularis canadensis Snapdragon Family May - June

The common name comes from an old European belief that cattle grazing on the Old World species would get lice. Flowers are strongly two-lipped with two of the five united petals forming an arched top. Usually yellow, they are often-times tinged with red. Stems are short and plants are tufted from a rootstock. Often the roots are associated with the roots of other plants. Common in the Eastern United States, this herbaceous perennial reaches the eastern part of the high plains, particularly in low, moist prairie.

1x Van Bruggen photo

SMALL-FLOWERED BUTTERCUP

Ranunculus abortivus Buttercup Family May

The yellow flowers of this buttercup are less than ½ inch in diameter. During and after flowering, the stems of this plant elongate and branch, reaching up to 18 inches tall. The basal leaves are rounded in outline and the stem leaves are deeply three- or five-parted. The fruiting heads are typical of the buttercup family, having many achenes crowded on the receptacle. The Small-Flowered Buttercup is common in alluvial woods and thickets over the eastern plains.

3x Van Bruggen photo

YELLOW WATER CROWFOOT

Ranunculus flabellaris Buttercup Family May - June

The vegetative parts of this aquatic buttercup are mostly below the water level. Leaves are divided into many linear segments and even the submersed ones effectively catch many of the sun's rays for manufacturing food. The Yellow Water Crowfoot grows in quiet water of ponds and lakes throughout the northern plains. Rooted in the mud, it grows in large patches and forms an attractive appearance when in flower. It reproduces by seed, by fragments that are carried by waterfowl, and by the offshoots of the perennial roots.

1/6x Van Bruggen photo

NARROW-LEAVED MUSINEON

Musineon tenuifolium Parsley Family May - June

This member of the parsley family is relatively common in the Black Hills. It grows in more rocky places than the Leafy Musineon (see page 22). It also lacks a main stem above ground. The narrow, linearly dissected leaves arise directly from the root crown. Individual flowers, very small and borne in tight clusters, may vary in color from bright yellow to off-white. Although bitter, the roots of this plant were used as a survival food by American Indians during harsh winters.

1/3x Van Bruggen photo

BRITTLE PRICKLYPEAR

Opuntia fragilis Cactus Family May - July

This cactus is appropriately named, for the stems are fragile, breaking at the narrow point where they join each other. Such brittleness has great survival benefit because it enables the plant to reproduce vegetatively; the piece of broken stem simply roots in a new location. This is the only pricklypear in the northern plains that has cylindrical joints instead of flat ones. Because the succulent plants are small, they are difficult to find in the prairie grasslands except when the pale yellow to orange flowers are present. The fruits of this perennial are dry and not edible.

1x Stockert photo

WESTERN WALLFLOWER

Erysimum asperum Mustard Family May - July

One of the scientific names for the Mustard Family is **Cruciferae** which originates from the word "cross," referring to the arrangement of the four flower petals. The showy, yellow petals of this biennial or short-lived perennial are each up to ½ inch long. Its fruits mature into conspicuous, four-angled pods up to 4 inches in length. The stiff, unbranched stems have downy hairs, giving it a grayish appearance. The long, narrow leaves tend to curve downward. The herb is widespread in dry or sandy prairie in the central and western states.

1x Stockert photo

WESTERN SALSIFY

Tragopogon dubius Aster Family May - August

A native herb of Europe, the deep taproot of this perennial allows it to compete successfully on dry prairie, waste ground and road sides. The pale-yellow flower heads, 2 or more inches across, grow singly at the ends of stems that are 1 to 3 feet tall. With fruiting heads which produce seeds with "parachutes," it is closely related to dandelions (**Taraxacum** sp.). Young plants have been used as potherbs and as greens. The coagulated, milky juice in the stems was considered by Indians to be a remedy for indigestion.

1/2x Stockert photo

TUMBLEMUSTARD

Sisymbrium altissimum Mustard Family May - September

An undesirable herb of fields and waste places, this winter annual begins its growth in the fall and eventually obtains a height of 3 feet or more. The leaves of the irregularly branched plant are linearly divided. After blooming, many long seed pods develop. Late in the growing season, the plant breaks off at ground level and is blown by the wind, spreading seeds which infest cultivated areas. Prairie tribes and early pioneers used the seeds for flavoring foods. Indians also ground them into meal which was used in making gruel (a liquid food made by boiling).

2x Stockert photo

STEMLESS HYMENOXYS

Hymenoxys acaulis Aster Family mid May - July

The word **acaulis**, meaning "stemless," refers to the leafless stalks, or scapes, which bear the flower heads. These blossoms are slightly over 2 inches in diameter. The yellow, ray florets have three prominent "teeth" at their ends. The leaves of this prairie perennial are lance-shaped or oblong, and grow in a cluster at soil level. Plants are usually less than a foot tall. Although rare in North Dakota, the herb is frequently seen in dry places in other areas of the plains states.

1/3x Stockert photo

COMMON MARSH-MARIGOLD

Caltha palustris Buttercup Family late May - June

The name "Marigold" is a misnomer in this case because it is more appropriately applied to members of the Aster Family. Not widely common throughout the northern plains, this perennial herb is, however, abundant in marshes and at the bases of seepage slopes in the eastern Dakotas. The flowers, up to 2 inches across, are strikingly waxy yellow. Lacking petals, the showy structures are actually sepals. The Dakota Sioux ate the new spring growth as greens. When boiled, it served as a potherb.

1/2x Van Bruggen photo

PRAIRIE GROUNDSEL

Senecio plattensis Aster Family late May - June

Of the more than 20 kinds of groundsel, or ragwort, as they are sometimes called, this is one of the most common in the prairie. The vegetation of this perennial herb has a cottony layer of hairs on its surface. Up to 10 flower heads cluster at the top of stems which grow to about 18 inches tall. A toxin produced by some groundsels causes liver damage. This condition is called stomach staggers in grazing animals. The various groundsels are hard to tell apart because of their similarity in appearance.

1x Stockert photo

MISSOURI PINCUSHION

Coryphantha missouriensis Cactus Family late May - June

The light yellow flowers of this almost spherical cactus betray its presence, for when not in flower, it is difficult to find among prairie grasses as only the upper portion protrudes above the prairie turf. The succulent stem, about 1 to 3 inches in diameter, is densely covered with spines. The small, rounded fruits are green until the following spring when they mature and turn scarlet. They nestle within the spines resembling eggs in a nest, hence another common name, Birds Nest Cactus. Usually growing in clusters of two to six, it is frequently found in dry prairies.

1/2x Stockert photo

STIFFSTEM FLAX

Linum rigidum Flax Family late May - August

The flowers of this prairie native open in the early forenoon but wither and fall off when the sun becomes hot. The herbs are annual and have slender, branched stems about 1 foot tall. The leaves are long and narrow. Seeds are formed in small, hard capsules that are yellow and split when mature. Several native flax species have been responsible for livestock poisoning. The poison is a cyanide compound that interferes with cellular respiration.

3x Stockert photo

YELLOW LADY SLIPPER

Cypripedium calceolus Orchid Family June

This well-known orchid is wide spread in North America as well as in Asia and Europe. In our area it is fairly common in rich woods of the Black Hills. The single stemmed plant grows up to 2 feet tall with several broad leaves. Usually one, but sometimes two, striking yellow flowers last for several weeks. The slipper, or lip, is up to 2 inches long. The lateral petals are spirally twisted and may be brown or greenish-yellow. Enjoy this orchid where it is found because it cannot be transplanted successfully.

1/2x Van Bruggen photo

NORTHERN GREEN ORCHID

Habenaria hyperborea Orchid Family June - July

Some of the orchids are not as showy as others. This one has small yellow-green flowers less than one inch long arranged in a tight spike about 6 inches long. The lip is less than ½ inch in length. In the northern plains this orchid is usually less than 2 feet tall. It grows in low, moist places in woods of the Black Hills and meadows elsewhere in the region. Oftentimes it occurs in dense stands but is not noticed because of the small, inconspicuous flowers and its small stature.

2/3x Van Bruggen photo

YELLOW PAINTED-CUP

Castilleja sulphurea Snapdragon Family June - July

The leafy bracts beneath the tight spike of flowers on the Yellow Painted-Cup remain for many weeks after the flowers mature. Typical of the painted-cups, the small, irregularly shaped flowers are highly adapted for insect pollination. A perennial herb, this one grows from a woody base. Stems are about 18 inches tall with many lance-shaped leaves. It is particularly common in meadows and open wooded hillsides of the Black Hills, but is uncommon elsewhere.

2/3x Van Bruggen photo

PALE MOUNTAIN-DANDELION

Agoseris glauca Aster Family June - July

The flower heads of this perennial bloom before the prairie grasses grow tall enough to obscure them. As in Common Dandelion (see page 23), all of the sometimes reddish blossoms are really many strap-like ray florets which form heads at the ends of leafless stems. The plant has milky juice in the stems. Its narrow, waxy-whitened leaves grow in a crowded rosette at the base of the herb. It sends a slender taproot deep and grows in moist areas of prairie swales, occurring more commonly westward.

1x Van Bruggen photo

DESERT PRINCESPLUME

Stanleya pinnata Mustard Family June - July

Bright yellow, stalked flowers and drooping pods on 3-foot, waxy stems make this sometimes-woody-based herb, or subshrub, a conspicuous sentinel of dry prairie knolls. The flowering plumes form as a result of continued growth of the stem tips. The stems bear symmetrically-lobed leaves which are common of many members of the Mustard Family. This perennial is well-known by ranchers as an indicator of soils containing selenium, a poisonous element which is easily absorbed by some plants. Although the plant accumulates selenium, animals do not eat enough to be poisoned.

1/6x Kravig photo

SILKTOP DALEA

Dalea aurea Legume Family June - July

The blossoms of this perennial open from the base to the top of the dense spike over a 4 to 6 week period. Each spike is up to 3 inches long and over ½ inch wide. The leaves, typical of the Legume Family, are made up of many, small, egg-shaped leaflets. Plains Indians crushed the leaves to prepare a drink for relieving colic and dysentery. Also called Silktop Indigobush, it has a woody base and grows on dry slopes and hillsides. Though often seen in the north central plains, it has not been reported from North Dakota.

1x Van Bruggen photo

ROUNDLEAF MONKEY FLOWER

Mimulus glabratus var. *fremontii* Snapdragon Family - July

The leaves of the Roundleaf Monkey Flower are characteristically rounded in outline, slightly toothed on their margins, and sessile on the stem. Plants are rooted in the mud of shallow water with the stems floating to the surface. Flowers are yellow to white, with petals about ½ inch long. They extend several inches above the water level and are easily seen. This plant occurs throughout the Great Plains in springs, creeks and ponds. It is spread by migrating waterfowl that eat or otherwise carry seeds from one place to another. A closely related species of monkey flower follows on the next page.

1x Van Bruggen photo

TICKSEED

Coreopsis palmata Aster Family July

A native of the true prairie in the eastern part of the Great Plains, this tickseed has narrow, three-parted leaves that are scattered on the stems. At flowering time the plants may be 2 to 3 feet tall. This plant gets its common name from the fact that the seed-like fruits or achenes are "bug-like," which is the meaning of the Greek word *Coreopsis*.

1/3x Van Bruggen photo

BRACTED UMBRELLA PLANT

Eriogonum flavum Buckwheat Family July - August

The many small, yellow flowers in a tight umbel and the leafy bracts immediately below make this prairie native attractive and easily recognized. It has a woody taproot that grows down to 8 or more feet below the soil surface. Eroded clay bluffs and exposed knolls are favorite habitats for this plant. There are over 20 species of umbrella plant in the Great Plains and they are commonly encountered in the western part of the northern plains. North American Indians collected the roots as a winter survival food.

1/3x Van Bruggen photo

MATCHBRUSH

Gutierrezia sarothrae Aster Family July - August

The thin, yellow to brown bases of this shrub that become woody give this common prairie native the name Matchbrush. Much branched, it grows to 2 or more feet tall on dry hillsides throughout the Great Plains. The leaves are narrow and have small, resinous dots. Individual flower heads are less than ¼ inch across. In winter Matchbrush serves as browse for mammals that live on the plains. Indians also used the plants for brooms, fuel and thatching.

3/4x Van Bruggen photo

YELLOW MONKEY FLOWER

Mimulus guttatus Snapdragon Family July - August

Swampy areas, potholes of the prairie, and springy areas in the western plains often have Yellow Monkey Flowers growing at their margins. Rooted in the mud, the stems extend above the water level or grow in patches adjacent to the water. The leaves are rounded, toothed and without stalks. Yellow flowers up to an inch in length, with a prominent, bearded area in the throat, top the stem. The term monkey flower refers to the "face-like" appearance of the flower.

3/4x Van Bruggen photo

FIVE-NERVED HELIANTHELLA

Helianthella quinquenervis Aster Family July - August

Two characteristics distinguish this tall, yellow-flowered perennial. The long, stalked flower head is nodded to the side and the principal leaves are prominently five-nerved. The name *Helianthella* means "sunflower like." However, the central disk of flowers on the head is yellow and not brown as in the Common Sunflower. Five-nerved Helianthella is a native of the mountainous regions west of the plains and is also found along streams in meadows of the Black Hills.

1/6x Van Bruggen photo

BUTTER-AND-EGGS

Linaria vulgaris Snapdragon Family June - September

This perennial owes it common name to the color of its blossoms. The flower structure is similar to that of the garden snapdragons and, like them, is highly adapted for insect pollination. One of the petals is modified, forming a long, downward projecting spur which contains a nectary. Unbranched stems grow up to 1 or 2 feet from a dense root system. The narrow leaves are numerous. Introduced from Europe, it is now widely established as a roadside herb. It commonly escapes from garden cultivation and forms large patches several yards in diameter.

1x Van Bruggen photo

UPRIGHT PRAIRIE-CONEFLOWER

Ratibida columnifera Aster Family June - September

A perennial with a spreading root system, this herb grows to 3 feet tall. The few, linearly dissected leaves are covered with a dense layer of hairs. "Coneflower" refers to the column, or cone, of tiny tubular flowers in the center of the flower head. At maturity these become single-seeded fruits, called achenes, which are similar to sunflower seeds. Prairie Indians gathered the heads during flowering time and made a tea-like beverage from them. Common in the Central States, the plant is one of our dominant prairie species.

1x Stockert photo

LEAFY SPURGE

Euphorbia podperae Spurge Family June - September

Leafy Spurge has been known as a toxic plant for several hundred years. A native of Eurasia, it has become naturalized in most of North America east of the Rockies. The herb is common on roadsides, in fields, and in other disturbed areas. Several states list this perennial as one of their 10 most noxious weeds. Growing in large, dense patches from a deep, bulb-like root, or rhizome system, it is difficult to eradicate. The prominent, yellowish parts are leafy bracts which are located just below the non-showy flowers.

1/3x Van Bruggen photo

BUFFALOBUR

Solanum rostratum Nightshade Family June - October

Buffalobur inhabits overgrazed pastures which have some nitrate reserves. An annual herb, it grows 1 to 2 feet tall. Its leaves are deeply divided with rounded lobes and look like those of the garden watermelon. The flowers resemble tomato or potato blossoms. Spiny capsules develop after flowering and hold many, small, black seeds. These are sporadically distributed when the plant breaks off at ground level, a common occurrence late in the growing season. Numerous spines which cover the vegetative parts discourage grazing animals. Several closely related species, including Black Nightshade (**S. nigrum**), are very poisonous.

1x Stockert photo

PRAIRIE DOGWEED

Dyssodia papposa Aster Family June - October

Sandy areas, roadsides, and prairie dog towns are common habitats for this ill-smelling annual. It is frequent throughout South Dakota, Nebraska, and to the west and east of these states. The herb produces many, small, hard, non-splitting fruits, each with one seed. Leaves are deeply cut into long, narrow, compound segments. The bitter odor emitted from small, yellow glands that dot the leaves irritates the nose. Plains Indians snuffed the pulverized leaves and tops to cause nosebleeds which supposedly relieved headaches. The low and much branched plants are avoided by grazing animals.

5x Stockert photo

CURLYCUP GUMWEED

Grindelia squarrosa Aster Family June - November

This much-branched biennial invades disturbed areas in the plains. Both the leaves and the curved bracts of the yellow flower heads exude a sticky material from minute glands. After flowering, tiny seeds mature, each with an awn, or protruding bristle, which aids in distribution by the wind. Dakota Indians prepared a decoction of the plant for treating children with colic. Other plains tribes extracted the gummy material for use against asthma and bronchitis. Early pioneers used the herb as a treatment for whooping cough and as an ingredient for asthma cigarettes.

1x Stockert photo

PLAINS PRICKLYPEAR

Opuntia polyacantha Cactus Family mid June - July

The term "pricklypear" is generally used for cacti that have flat, jointed stems. Leaves are very short-lived. They drop off soon after the formation of a new portion of the stem which takes over the functions of the leaves. The thick stem also serves as a succulent, water storage organ. The blossoms of this perennial are large, waxy, and usually yellow with reddish centers. When in bloom, the pricklypears are a mass of yellow on dry buttes or mesas. The red, pulpy fruits of this species are edible and tasty. Early settlers made jellies and jams from them.

1/2x Stockert photo

COMMON SUNFLOWER

Helianthus annuus Aster Family late June - October

Although it is the state flower of Kansas, this annual is found from the East Coast to the foothills of the Rocky Mountains. The herbs vary in height from 1 to 10 feet and bear flower heads that are 2 to 6 inches in diameter. Several varieties are cultivated for their seeds which, when roasted, are eaten like peanuts. Historically, the seeds served as a favorite food of the Plains Indians who roasted and ground them for bread and gruel, or extracted the oils for use in cooking.

1/2x Van Bruggen photo

FRINGED LOOSESTRIFE

Lysimachia ciliata Primrose Family July - August

The deep yellow, five-parted flowers of this perennial typify the loosestrifes. Short hairs edge the petals and leafstalks. The petals last only a few days. After they fall, berries develop, each containing several angular seeds. Stems grow 1 to 3 feet tall, bearing broad leaves that are opposite. The herb is found in thickets, rich woods, shores, and other moist areas of the eastern plains and further eastward.

1x Van Bruggen photo

GRAYHEAD PRAIRIE-CONEFLOWER

Ratibida pinnata Aster Family July - August

A tall and erect perennial, this prairie-coneflower commonly grows up to 4 feet or more. It is usually branched in the upper half. The center of the flower head, the disk, is dome-like. The outer 10 to 12 petal-like ray florets droop almost as soon as they develop fully. The large leaves are pinnately divided, which means the leaflets are on each side of a common stem. It is a showy, midsummer herb of roadsides and edges of thickets in the Dakotas and Nebraska and eastward.

1/4x Van Bruggen photo

COMPASS-PLANT

Silphium laciniatum Aster Family July - August

Sunlight causes the large, irregularly lobed leaves at the base of this perennial to grow with their edges running generally in a north-south direction. Each leaf is up to a foot long and 6 inches wide. The yellow flower heads grow right from the stout stem which may be as high as 4 to 6 feet. Because the juice in the stem is resinous, the plant is also called Rosinweed. Prairie Indians chewed the thick, juicy stem, which, at first, tastes bitter but becomes tolerable after some chewing. This herb prefers the prairies of the eastern plains.

1/4x Van Bruggen photo

CUP ROSINWEED

Silphium perfoliatum Aster Family July - August

Two characteristics identify this coarse perennial. First, the fused bases of the opposite main leaves form cups around the stem, and second, the stem is angular and almost square. These herbs reach 6 feet tall of more with several branches at the top, each with two to four flower heads which are nearly 3 inches in diameter. The plant is frequently found in moist, open places and in roadside ditches of the eastern part of the Great Plains.

1/4x Van Bruggen photo

FLOWER-OF-AN-HOUR

Hibiscus trionum Mallow Family July - August

The genus **Hibiscus** has many striking flowers, both wild and cultivated. Most are native to the tropics, especially Hawaii. All have flaring, colorful petals around a central column which is filled with pollen sacs and topped by the pollen-receiving surface, the stigma. Flowers of this species open for only a few hours each morning. The leaves are deeply cut into three parts. The herb grows to less than 2 feet tall. A native of Europe, Flower-of-an-Hour is now a common annual of fields and abandoned cultivated areas in the eastern plains.

2/3x Van Bruggen photo

BLACKEYED-SUSAN

Rudbeckia hirta Aster Family July - August

Many Midwest meadows in August are literally yellow with the flowers of this biennial or short-lived perennial. Widespread in the United States, the herb grows well in disturbed ground and on roadsides. Plants have harsh hairs on their surfaces. Stems are 1 to 2 feet tall. The 2½-inch flower heads have petal-like, yellowish-orange ray florets which bleach somewhat toward maturity. Several forms of **Rudbeckia** have been adapted for cultivation and are called Golden Glow.

1x Van Bruggen photo

COMMON EVENING-PRIMROSE

Oenothera biennis Evening-Primrose Family July - September

The four yellow petals of this biennial herb are attached to the top of the ovary. Flowers are arranged in a spike-like fashion on stems which may grow up to 5 feet tall. Late in the season there may be over 50 oval fruits clustered along the upper 18 inches of the stem. These pods release their many seeds over a considerable period of time. Inhabiting waste places and roadsides, it grows in most of temperate North America and Canada.

1x Stockert photo

ROUGH OX-EYE

Heliopsis helianthoides Aster Family July - September

This perennial with its paired, opposite leaves and smooth stem reaching up 2 to 5 feet looks very much like a sunflower. The term **helianthoides** means "sunflower-like." Blooming individually for a considerable time, the 2- to 3-inch flower heads have a center disk of small florets which is conical. This feature along with its opposite leaves distinguishes this herb from the sunflowers. Rough Ox-Eye is common in prairie remnants along roads and at the edges of thickets in the northern plains.

1/4x Van Bruggen photo

TENPETAL BLAZINGSTAR

Mentzelia decapetala Loasa Family July - September

Occurring on dry hillsides and eroded clay banks of the northern plains, this biennial has stout stems and deep roots. The herbs grow up to 2 feet, with harshly toothed leaves up to 8 inches long. The yellowish, cream-colored flowers open in the evening and are pollinated by night-flying insects, primarily moths. Its flower structure is similar to that of cactus. The fruit is a pod up to 2 inches long, containing many flattened seeds. Prairie Indians squeezed the juice from the stems for treatment of fevers.

1/2x Stockert photo

MISSOURI GOLDENROD

Solidago missouriensis Aster Family July - September

This perennial herb is probably the most common goldenrod in the northern plains. The brown to green stems have a polished appearance and rise from creeping, underground roots. Narrow leaves crowd the stem. The flower heads grow on ends of branches that curve out and down from the main stem. Reaching a height of 8 to 30 inches, this early blooming goldenrod grows in a variety of habitats including dry prairie and other open places.

1/2x Van Bruggen photo

JERUSALEM ARTICHOKE

Helianthus tuberosus Aster Family July - August

The term Jerusalem in the common name of this sunflower is erroneous and is a corruption of the Italian word **girasole** meaning "turning to the sun." The word artichoke, however, is quite appropriate. The roots of this plant have enlarged, tuberous regions that are rich in starches and quite edible. This wildflower is native to the entire central part of North America and was cultivated by Indian tribes long before Europeans came to this continent. It grows in low meadows and other moist places. The stems reach 5 feet and are topped by bright yellow heads.

1/5x Van Bruggen photo

OWL'S CLOVER

Orthocarpus luteus Snapdragon Family July - August

This member of the snapdragon family is an annual plant which grows in sandy prairie over the western plains. The common name refers to the upright or owl-like nature of the fruits. The small, two-lipped flowers are about ½ inch long and arranged in dense spikes. Stems are erect and reach 12 inches or more in height. Its leaves are narrow and pressed close to the stem. Many hundreds of small seeds are produced by each plant, insuring the growth of new plants the following year.

1/2x Van Bruggen photo

STIFF GOLDENROD

Solidago rigida Aster Family August

The prairie in August is "at attention" with the erect and rigid stems of this perennial goldenrod. The stems are stout, unbranched, and up to 3 feet tall. It is also distinguished by the dense, crown-like cluster of flowers topping the stem. The thick, woody roots are branched and grow deeply into the prairie turf. Stiff Goldenrod inhabits upland prairies from Minnesota to Texas and west to the Rocky Mountains.

1/4x Van Bruggen photo

COMMON MULLEIN

Verbascum thapsus Snapdragon Family July-September

Native of Europe, this plant was brought by man to many of the places he has disturbed. A biennial, it produces a basal rosette of large, thick leaves the first year and an erect, thick stem up to 6 feet tall the second year. The yellow flowers are up to 1 inch wide and form a long, dense spike at the top of the fleshy stem. Dead stems may stand erect for several years after flowering. A familiar herb of rocky soil, hillsides, and over-grazed pastures, it is thoroughly established in this region.

1/2x Van Bruggen photo

PUNCTURE-VINE

Tribulus terrestris Caltrop Family July - October

The small flowers of this annual are open only in the morning. The fruits, or "stickers," are distinctive because each of their five parts has two heavy, sharp, ½-inch spines that easily puncture bicycle tires. The flat vine forms a mat the size of a square yard or larger. It grows on sandy or thin soil, and is abundant on railroad ballasts and roadsides. A native of Europe, this herb now extends from Eastern United States to the western edge of the high plains and the southwestern states.

2x Stockert photo

IRONPLANT GOLDENWEED

Haplopappus spinulosus Aster Family July - October

There are over 25 species of goldenweed in the Great Plains; all are characterized by dense clusters of yellow flowers at the ends of tough, wiry stems. This species has compound leaves whose long segments are spine-tipped, hence the term *spinulosus*. As as result, grazing animals avoid the plant. A hardy perennial, it grows in dry prairie from a woody base and deep root system.

1x Stockert photo

MAXIMILIAN SUNFLOWER

Helianthus maximiliana Aster Family late July - September

This tall, many-flowered perennial with flexible stems was named after the German prince, Maximilian, who made several botanical explorations in North and South America during the early 1800's. The herb is a conspicuous inhabitant of swales and other low places of the plains, where it is usually associated with tall, prairie grasses. A good identifying characteristic is its long, narrow leaves that fold into a V-shape, curving outward from the stem. Each flower head is 3 or more inches across. Prairie Indians collected the short rootstocks for food.

1/3x Van Bruggen photo

RUBBER RABBITBRUSH

Chrysothamnus nauseosus Aster Family late July - October

The generic name, meaning "golden bush," refers to the many, small, yellow florets that cluster at the ends of woody branches. Usually each clump of stems attains 1 to 3 feet in height. When blooming, it is the most conspicuous flower in many areas during September. It is a common inhabitant of dry slopes and eroding bluffs in the western, arid parts of the Dakotas, Nebraska, and further west. Prairie Indians used the shrub for medicines, dyes, and fuel. It also serves as a winter browse for pronghorn, deer and elk.

1/2x Stockert photo

HAIRY GOLDASTER

Chrysopsis villosa Aster Family late July - October

Although the flower head of this perennial herb resembles that of the asters, there are several dissimilarities. The most obvious one is that the ray florets are yellow, unlike the usually white to purple blossoms of the aster. **Villosa** means "hairy," which refers to the covering of hairs on the stem and leaf surfaces. Stems grow 6 inches to 2 feet tall, depending on the moisture available. Its deep rootstocks are an adaptation to dry prairie habitats. This goldaster is common in the western plains and Black Hills, but rare in the eastern part of the Dakotas and Nebraska.

1/2x Stockert photo

SAWTOOTH SUNFLOWER

Helianthus grosseserratus Aster Family August - September

One of 16 species of sunflower native to the northern plains, this coarse perennial inhabits open bottomlands and ditches along roads. The lance-shaped leaves of the herb have wide "teeth" along the edges. The branched stems, varying from 3 to 10 feet tall, bear flower heads that are 3 or more inches across. The center disk is yellow and smaller than the brownish-purple disk of Common Sunflower (see page 23).

1/4x Van Bruggen photo

SHOWY PARTRIDGE-PEA

Cassia fasciculata Legume Family August - September

A common herb of low, sandy areas along rivers and streams, this annual ranges from Massachusetts to Texas. It is frequently seen on sand bars along the Missouri River. The erect stems grow 1 to 3 feet high, bearing compound leaves, each with 8 to 12 pairs of leaflets. The flowers have an irregular symmetry, meaning that each petal has a somewhat different shape and orientation than the others. Seeds are produced in small pods and are forcibly expelled when mature. Weakly toxic to animals, it and other closely related species are also cathartic.

1/2x Van Bruggen photo

ROUGH RATTLESNAKE-ROOT

Prenanthes aspera Aster Family August - September

The underground parts of this perennial are very bitter and were believed effective as a treatment for snakebites. This is yet another example of the idea that bad taste indicates medicinal value, which is not true. Stems are tall, up to 5 feet, with creamy-yellow flower heads arranged along the upper part as shown. Large, oval, wide-tipped leaves with short, stiff, surface hairs grow at the base of the stem. This herb occasionally inhabits moist swales in the eastern plains.

1/2x Van Bruggen photo

SHOWY GOLDENROD

Solidago speciosa Aster Family August - September

Speciosa, meaning "beautiful," is a good description for this goldenrod. Plants, commonly 1 to 2 feet tall and solitary, grow from a stout, woody root. The stiff, erect stems bear many leaves that are larger toward the base. The flower cluster, or inflorescence, is a tight, cylindrical mass of yellow heads, each usually with five large ray florets. This perennial herb inhabits open thickets and rocky woods as well as the high plains and Black Hills.

1/2x Van Bruggen photo

CANADA GOLDENROD

Solidago canadensis Aster Family August - September

Of the more than 25 species of goldenrod native to the high plains, this book includes only five of the most common. Although some are quite distinctive, most are hard to tell apart. The yellow flower heads of Canada Goldenrod have the characteristic arrangement and shape pictured. The leaves have three prominent veins and are progressively smaller toward the top of the herb. The stems and leaves look grayish-green because of their short surface hairs. This perennial is common in thickets, in open fields, and on roadsides.

1/3x Van Bruggen photo

GRAY GOLDENROD

Solidago nemoralis Aster Family August - September

The flower clusters of this drought-resistant goldenrod are generally arranged along one side of a curved stem. The herb grows from a thick root stock, usually to a height of less than a foot but may grow as high as 2 feet. The bottom leaves soon die, leaving a barren lower stem with short leaves toward the top. This perennial favors dry places on the high plains. Indians used the flowering of goldenrod as an indication of when their corn was beginning to ripen.

1/2x Van Bruggen photo

SILVERWEED

Potentilla anserina Rose Family May - June

There are 18 or more species of Potentilla in the Great Plains. Some are shrubby or with woody bases but most are annual to perennial herbs. All have leaves with 3 to many leaflets. This early spring flower of the wet meadows of prairie or along streams has leaves to 6 inches long, composed of 15 or more leaflets. The undersides of the leaves have long, white hairs, hence the name Silverweed. It is perennial and has runners like strawberry. The striking yellow flowers are on naked stalks or peduncles from the runners or from the main plant. This plant's roots were used by Native Americans and early settlers as a spring purgative. The dried herb, in boiling water, was used as a gargle for sore throats.

2/3x Van Bruggen photo

YELLOW STARGRASS

Hypoxis hirsuta Lily Family May - June

This small, grass-like plant grows from a deep-seated corm, a fleshy stem shaped like a bulb. The leaves grow directly from the corm to about 6 inches. The name hirsuta refers to the fine, scattered hairs on the stem and leaves. The star-shaped flowers are up to 1 inch across, in small clusters on thread-like stems that are shorter than the leaves. The 6 perianth parts, all petal-like, spread to form a 6-pointed star. This is typical of the flowers in the Lily Family. Yellow stargrass is found in meadows of moist prairie in the eastern part of the Northern Plains west to the Sandhills of Nebraska and South Dakota. Native Americans used the bulb-like corms as a treatment for ulcers.

1x Van Bruggen photo

PLAINS YELLOW PRIMROSE

Calylophus serrulatus Evening-primrose Family June - July

One of the most common and wide-ranging yellow flowers of the Northern Plains is this member of the Evening Primrose Family. The stems grow from a deep, woody root and vary from 4 to 10 inches tall. The narrow, serrate-margined leaves are from 1 to 2 inches long. Usually many flowers are produced in the upper leaf axils, bright yellow with petals up to one-half inch long. The 4 yellow petals, two each across from each other, are produced at the top of a 4-parted tubular ovary. This is characteristic of this family (See Oenothera and Epilobium). Plains Yellow Primrose is found in rich prairie, to gravelly soils and open woodlands over our area.

3/4x Van Bruggen photo

BLANKET-FLOWER

Gaillardia aristata Aster Family June - July

Blanket Flower is showy in the prairie in June and July. It never is very abundant. Simple to several-branched stems grow to one and one-half feet tall, topped by a single flower head. The rayflowers are yellow and notched at their ends, but reddish to lavender near their bases. The disk, or center of the flower head, is purple early, becoming densely hairy towards maturity. Its leaves and stem have rough, long hairs, from which the name **aristata** is derived. A perennial from a deep taproot, Blanket-flower is widely distributed in prairies over the Northern Plains.

1/4x Van Bruggen photo

TUFTED LOOSESTRIFE

Lysimachia thyrsiflora Primrose Family June - July

A distinctive feature of the Tufted Loosestrife are the stalked tufts or clusters of yellow flowers arising from the axils of leaves near the medial portion of the stem. The stems are shiny, mostly without hairs, and have lance-shaped leaves. Plants grow from a densely creeping underground rhizome system and may be 2 feet tall.

The individual flowers have narrow yellow petals with elongate stamens giving the tufts of flowers a bristly appearance. Tufted loosestrife is widely spread over the Northern Plains in swampy or marshy soils and along lake shores.

1/3x Van Bruggen photo

PLAINS COREOPSIS

Coreopsis tinctoria Aster Family July - August

This annual plant is widespread over the western Plains. In seasonally damp places, such as along roadsides or in gravelly or sandy ponds in prairie, a solid bed of this showy wildflower up to several hundred yards long is not uncommon. The stems are much-branched, slender, to one and one-half feet tall, with narrow, divided leaves. Flower heads terminate the many branches. The ray flowers are bright yellow with usually 4 lobes. The bases of the ray flowers have a reddish spot, which, along with the disk flowers, also red, make a contrasting, showy appearance. This species is cultivated in eastern states as an ornamental.

1/2x Van Bruggen photo

GOLDEN GLOW

Rudbeckia laciniata Aster Family July - September

Golden Glow, or Coneflower, as it is sometimes called, is a coarse, weedy perennial up to 5 feet or more tall. It grows from a woody base. All but uppermost leaves are laciniate, or deeply-divided along the entire stem. The yellow ray flowers on the flowerhead are 2-3 inches long, and usually droop downward. The central disk flowers are also yellow, but become gray-colored at maturity. Native Americans used the flowers of several species of **Rudbeckia** for dyes, and various concoctions of this species were used as a tonic. Golden Glow is common in moist, alluvial places over the Great Plains.

1/6x Van Bruggen photo

SNEEZEWEED

Helenium autumnale Aster Family August - September

Where the common name Sneezeweed originated is perhaps lost in antiquity. However, several related species are known to be toxic to grazing animals. The scientific name **Helenium**, from the Greek, celebrates the memory of Helen of Troy. The species name **autumnale** refers to the time of flowering, in early fall. Sneezeweed is a perennial from stringy rhizomes with stout stems 2 feet or more tall. The leaves are lance-shaped, with their bases continuing down the stem as small flanges or wings. Another distinguishing feature is the prominent dome of disk flowers on the flower head, about the same yellow color as the ray flowers. Sneezeweed is found sporadically in moist soils of alluvial woods or open places over the northern plains.

1/5x Van Bruggen photo

FOURPOINT EVENING PRIMROSE

Oenothera rhombipetala Evening-Primrose Family July - September

There are over 20 species of white and yellow evening primroses in the Great Plains. This one has the characteristic 4 petals that are somewhat rhombic in shape. Plants are mostly biennial, producing a spike of bright yellow flowers the second year. Stems are 2 feet or more tall, with many crowded leaves. The flowers open shortly before sunset. Each petal is about one-half inch long, bluntly tapered at each end. The central flower parts, the 8 stamens and 4-lobed stigma, are prominent and project well above the spread petals. Fourpoint Evening primrose is found in sandy prairie and on sand dunes in the Great Plains.

1/4x Van Bruggen photo

AMERICAN PLUM

Prunus americana Rose Family April - May

This wild plum is common in draws and thickets throughout the Midwest. The shrub-like trees are 6 to 10 feet tall. Older branches become somewhat spiny. The five-parted white flowers, each up to 1 inch wide, bloom in small clusters on second-year wood. The fruits turn reddish-orange, maturing in August and early September. Indians and early pioneers sought the fruits and ate them fresh, dried in the winter, or cooked as a sauce. Wild plum jam is unsurpassed on breakfast toast!

1/2x Van Bruggen photo

White Flowers

SNOW TRILLIUM

Trillium nivale Lily Family April

This was photographed in the second week of April where large snow banks on the northern slope of a ravine were melting. In 3 out of 12 years in this ravine, Snow Trillium was in bloom before the snow had disappeared. Only 3 or 4 inches tall, the herb has 3 leaves that radiate from the stem at one point and a single white flower at the top of the stem. A native of rich, loamy woods, this perennial reaches the eastern parts of the Dakotas and Nebraska, where the eastern deciduous woods give way to the prairies.

1/3x Van Bruggen photo

COMMON CHOKECHERRY

Prunus virginiana Rose Family April - May

This shrub may grow up to 20 feet or more and is often found in ravines and valleys. The fruits ripen in late July or early August to a dark purple, each one very tart with a single stone. Plains Indians dried the fruits for winter use and ground them up to make into cakes in the summer. They ground both fresh and dried fruits and mixed them with dried meat to make a popular food known as pemmican. Chokecherries make delicious jelly and jam.

1/4x Stockert photo

CANADA VIOLET

Viola canadensis Violet Family April - May

A native of Canada and northern United States, this perennial herb forms dense stands in shaded woods. Stems, up to 1 foot tall, bear broad, oval leaves with irregular teeth. The white flowers have pale lavender veins or outer edges and may turn purple as they age. Many seeds are produced that germinate easily in gardens. Indians ate the young leaves and stems as greens and also made a beverage of the flowers.

1/2x Van Bruggen photo

DUTCHMANS-BREECHES

Dicentra cucullaria Poppy Family April - June

The soft, green deeply-cut leaves and the arching stems of two to eight, nodding, white flowers provide for easy identification of Dutchmans-breeches. An early spring herb of loamy slopes in eastern timber, it is found occasionally in the woods of the eastern part of the Dakotas and Nebraska where prairie gradually becomes the dominant vegetation. This perennial grows up to 8 inches from grain-like tubers. The outer petals of each flower resemble two inverted sacs. The green fruits are shaped like, but smaller than, the pods of the garden green pea.

1/2x Van Bruggen photo

TUFTED EVENING-PRIMROSE

Oenothera caespitosa Evening-primrose Family April - August

Also known as Gumbo-lily, this hardy perennial of dry buttes and clay banks has large white flowers produced at ground level which turn pink and wilt in less than a day. This showy evening-primrose is frequently cultivated as an ornamental. Its fruiting pods, when mature, are up to 1 inch long. The principal leaves at the base of the stem are coarsely toothed. Prairie Indians cooked the stout taproots of this herb for food. They also prepared a decoction, a liquid preparation made by boiling, from the taproots for a treatment against coughs and other respiratory infections.

1/3x Stockert photo

RED PUSSYTOES

Antennaria rosea Aster Family May - June

Many of the pussytoes are dioecious, that is, the male plants and female plants grow separately. This is a photograph of a female plant. The leaf-like bracts surrounding the flower heads are tinged with pink. All of the pussytoes of the northern plains are perennials. They grow in large mats, spreading by runners. The leaves of this one are small and spoon-shaped, with a dense, white layer of hairs on both surfaces. The flowering stalks are about 5 inches tall with white and pink flower parts that are soft like the toes of a young kitten.

1x Van Bruggen photo

WATERLEAF

Hydrophyllum virginianum Waterleaf Family May - June

The common name of this woodland herb refers to the watery juice in the stems and leaves. The stems elongate rapidly in the spring and begin flowering before the overhead trees are fully in leaf. The flower clusters are dense and unroll as the individual flowers open. Their color may vary from white to pale lavender. Waterleaf grows in the eastern parts of the Dakotas and Nebraska where the woodlands meet the prairie. It is common in the central and eastern parts of the United States.

1/3x Van Bruggen photo

BLOODROOT

Sanguinaria canadensis Poppy Family April - May

Poppies the world over have colored or milky juice in various parts of the plant body. The Bloodroot is no exception. Its underground stems or rhizomes yield a blood-red juice when broken. Native American Indians used it as a dye. They named these dye-producing plants Puccoons (see page 24). The dainty, white flowers have 8 petals. The supporting flower stalks are naked and grow to a height of 8 inches in early spring. Later the leaves expand on stalks that grow directly from the underground stem. Bloodroot occurs in rich woods of eastern North and South Dakota but is rare in the Black Hills.

1/4x Van Bruggen photo

HOOD PHLOX

Phlox hoodii Phlox Family mid April - June

A low perennial with a dense, mat-like appearance, this herb is a showy plant on prairie knolls and exposed areas when in bloom. Resistant to drought because of a deep root system, it prefers dry and eroded areas where other plants cannot grow. The grayish leaves are pointed and up to ½ inch long. The flowers are white to light pink, or sometimes darker pink, and are relished by sheep. Common in the high plains, it is rare or absent in eastern North and South Dakota. Several native species of phlox are sold commercially for ornamental planting.

1x Stockert photo

SHADBLOW SERVICEBERRY

Amelanchier alnifolia Rose Family late April

Experts cannot agree on how to classify the eight or more North American serviceberries into proper species. This one, a small, shrubby tree that reaches 10 feet tall, grows in clumps or thickets on hillsides and on the edges of wooded ravines. The oval leaves appear after the plant flowers. Many birds and mammals eat the fruit clusters which taste remotely like apples but are mealy and dry. Indians used the twigs and bark for basketry and weaving.

1/3x Van Bruggen photo

COMMON STARLILY

Leucocrinum montanum Lily Family late April - June

This stemless perennial of plains and hillsides grows from several fleshy roots that are like coarse strings radiating out in several directions. All of the leaves are narrow and grasslike and arise from a short crown into a rosette. The word **Leucocrinum** comes from the Greek meaning "white lily." It refers to the white, star-shaped flowers that open at soil level. The fruiting capsule, about ½ inch long, forms just underground. The seeds of this herb will germinate successfully in cultivation.

1x Van Bruggen photo

DOWNY PAINTBRUSH

Castilleja sessiliflora Snapdragon Family late April - June

The early flowers are long and narrow and are highly adapted for insect pollination. The petals, varying from green to yellow, are almost hidden from view by conspicuous whitish-yellow, leafy bracts. A perennial herb, it is usually less than 1 foot tall and grows in clumps on dry prairie, ranging from Saskatchewan to Texas. Over 100 species occur in the Rocky Mountains and the Pacific Northwest. Many are partial root parasites of other plants.

1/2x Stockert photo

BALLHEAD IPOMOPSIS

Ipomopsis congesta Phlox Family late April - June

One of more than 25 species of the Phlox Family native to the western plains and Rocky Mountains, this densely hairy herb grows from a branched, woody root system to a height of less than one foot. White flowers, each ¼ inch wide, thickly cluster or congest as a rounded head at the top of the plant. This perennial prefers dry habitats such as the tops and edges of buttes. It will transplant easily to gardens. A number of closely related forms called **Gilias** are cultivated as ornamentals.

3x Stockert photo

FLESHY HAWTHORN

Crataegus succulenta Rose Family May

This small tree, which may grow to more than 10 feet tall, has many sharp, unbranched spines on the branches. The hairy leaves are round with sharp "teeth" called serrations. Arranged in terminal clusters, the white, five-petaled flowers are each about ½ inch across. Small, apple-like fruits mature in August, each containing three to five nutlets. Plains Indians ate these fruits after they were pounded into a meal and baked. Fleshy Hawthorn is frequent in steep-walled valleys and on the slopes and tops of ravines.

1/2x Van Bruggen photo

STARRY SOLOMONPLUME

Smilacina stellata Lily Family May - June

The small, six-petaled, white blossoms of this perennial form a simple cluster at the top of the stem. *Stellata*, meaning "star-shaped," refers to the contour of the flowers. The blooms are followed by green, black-striped berries that are about ¼ inch thick. Growing from a rooted fibrous rhizome (thickened underground stem), the 10 to 18-inch stems are zig-zagged with bright green, lanceolate leaves. Very common in thickets and woodlands in temperate North America, this herb is one of our better known spring flowers.

2x Stockert photo

TEXTILE ONION

Allium textile Lily Family May - June

Of the many species of wild onion, this is perhaps the most common on the north central prairie. The 15-inch plants grow from solitary, underground bulbs which are covered with fibrous, netted veins. The flower cluster, an umbel (fan-shaped), varies from white to deep pink. Prairie Indians ate many kinds of wild onions and prepared decoctions of the bulb juice for treating sore throats. They also dried the bulbs for future use as food and flavoring.

1/3x Stockert photo

GRASSY DEATHCAMASS

Zigadenus venenosus var. *gramineus* Lily Family May - June

Several North American species of deathcamass are among the most poisonous plants of the plains. An alkaloid is the toxic substance, producing symptoms similar to cyanide poisoning. The stems of this herbaceous perennial grow up to 2 feet from an onion-like bulb. Flowers are arranded in a loose spike. Each petal has a half-moon shaped gland at its base. The lack of an onion odor distinguishes deathcamass from the wild onions. However, there have been cases of poisoning in Indians and settlers who mistakenly ate them.

2x Stockert photo

COMMON COMANDRA

Comandra umbellata Sandalwood Family May - June

The stems of this perennial arise from an underground rhizome, or bulb-like root system, which attaches to the roots of various plants. Technically, it is called a hemi-parasite, or halfway parasite. Their roots are never well-developed. The herb does, however, have the ability to produce its own food photosynthetically. Clusters of flowers, usually whitish, develop at the tops of stems that only reach 4 to 6 inches tall. Widespread in the prairie where deep turf is available, it is also found under oak trees.

3x Stockert photo

WHITE PENSTEMON

Penstemon albidus Snapdragon Family May - June

More than 250 species of penstemon, also known as beardstongue, grow in North America. White Penstemon often inhabits exposed, dry prairie with calcium-bearing soil. Several stems about 10 inches high shoot from a woody rootstock. These stems are covered with short, soft hairs that are glandular. In contrast to other prairie penstemons which have various shades of red to blue flowers, this plant has inch-long, white blossoms. Their insides are bearded and often spotted with purple. An herbaceous perennial, this plant is found mainly in the high plains but does reach southward to Texas and New Mexico.

1x Stockert photo

NODDING WHITE TRILLIUM

Trillium cernuum Lily Family May - June

Three large leaves nearly hide the single white flower of this graceful, thin-stemmed herb of rich woods. **Cernuum**, meaning "nodding" or "curved downward," is a reference to the drooping flower that is about 2 inches across with petals and sepals each numbering three. The 12- to 18-inch stem grows rapidly from creeping rootstocks. Common in Eastern United States, this perennial ranges to the Red River Valley of North Dakota and into South Dakota and Iowa.

1/2x Van Bruggen photo

WILD LILY OF THE VALLEY

Maianthemum canadense Lily Family May - June

This common wildflower of woodlands, often pine or spruce woods, is found from Labrador to British Columbia and south throughout North America. It is also called the Canada Mayflower. It often is found in dense mats under trees where the stems spread by underground runners. Flower stalks are 3 to 8 inches tall and have two or three heart-shaped leaves that clasp the stem. Usually members of the lily family have flower parts in threes, but this one has them in twos and fours. In the northern plains it grows in the eastern Dakotas and in the Black Hills.

1/3x Van Bruggen photo

WHITE LOCOWEED

Oxytropis sericea Legume Family June

A close relative of the Lambert Crazyweed, White Locoweed is not as common. It grows in the western and southern parts of the northern plains. As the common name indicates, it possesses a toxic material that can cause poisoning in grazing livestock. The predominant color of the flowers is white, but often they are tinged with lavender. The flowering stalks are naked. Leaves are many-parted and arise from soil level as in the other members of the **Oxytropis** group.

1/3x Van Bruggen photo

PIN CHERRY

Prunus pensylvanica Rose Family June - July

The cherries and plums are very much alike when they flower. When they fruit, however, the plums have a groove on one side and a flattened stone. The cherries, on the other hand, have a stone that is smaller and spherical. Pin Cherry has a growth habit that is very similar to the wild plum. The shrubby trees are 6-10 feet tall with flower clusters similarly arranged, however, the flowers of the cherry are smaller. Pin Cherry makes good jam and was used by Indians in making pemmican. It grows in North Dakota and Minnesota and west to the Black Hills in the northern plains.

1/2x Van Bruggen photo

COMMON STRAWBERRY

Fragaria virginiana Rose Family May - June

Because of its similarity to cultivated forms, this wild strawberry needs little description. Cultivated strawberries were developed by hybrid crosses from several native stocks. This herb inhabits open areas and loamy woods from the East Coast to the Rockies and south to Oklahoma. The stems are very short and perennial. Most vegetative reproduction occurs by surface runners. Although it flowers in relatively large numbers, few fruits are set and they are much smaller than the cultivated varieties. Woodland Indians prized the fruits when available. They also prepared an infusion from the leaves which they drank as tea.

1/2x Van Bruggen photo

BRADBURY CRYPTANTHA

Cryptantha celosioides Borage Family May - September

This harsh, bristly biennial of prairie slopes and ridges has long, stiff hairs covering the stems and leaves which give it a grayish appearance. The conspicuous flowers are ½ inch or less in diameter and are arranged along short branches that become recurved, or curved downward. Also known as Butte Candle, this herb is an inhabitant of the western plains. It is common in the sandhills of Nebraska but is rare east of the Missouri River in the Dakotas. Grazing animals avoid it because of the spiny hairs.

1/4x Stockert photo

FIELD BINDWEED

Convolvulus arvensis Morning-glory Family May - September

Many farmers call this plant Creeping Jenny. Difficult to eradicate from fields because of deep, spreading roots, it can be destroyed only by heavy, repeated doses of weed killer. A native of Europe, this perennial has become naturalized in most of the United States and Canada. The pinkish-white petals are joined to form a funnel-shaped flower, typical of the Morning-glory Family. The leaves are somewhat arrow-shaped. Many states have the herb listed as one of their noxious weeds.

1/2x Stockert photo

LOW FLEABANE

Erigeron pumilus Aster Family mid May - June

The word **pumilus**, meaning "small," refers to the size of the herb. The stout, deep taproot is perennial and has the ability to persist in extremely dry places. Many glandular hairs cover the long, narrow leaves. Flower heads are approximately 1 inch in diameter. The ray florets, usually white, have narrow, strap-shaped petals. This characteristic, plus the presence of many leaf-like bracts at the base of the heads, distinguishes fleabanes from asters. Low Fleabane is commonly found in plains but not as far east as eastern Nebraska or the eastern Dakotas.

1/2x Stockert photo

RACEMED POISONVETCH

Astragalus racemosus Legume Family mid May - August

One of several **Astragalus** species poisonous to livestock, this herb accumulates selenium, which causes "blind staggers" and alkali disease in grazing animals. The coarse, erect stems bear yellowish-white flowers which are attached singly, each with its own small stalk. The plant grows in clumps from a stout taproot and reaches about 2 feet in height. This perennial has a wide geographic distribution in the northern plains and is considered to be a selenium indicator of soils where it is found.

2x Stockert photo

INLAND CEANOTHUS

Ceanothus herbaceus Buckthorn Family late May - June

This close relative of New Jersey Tea (**C. americanus**) is a bushy shrub which grows up to 2 feet. Preferring sandy or dry prairie hillsides and thicket edges, it is frequent in Nebraska and South Dakota, although it has not been reported in North Dakota. The small, white blossoms occur in a showy, dense cluster called a panicle. The leaves are ovate, or egg-shaped, with fine serrations. Young leaves and flowering stalks can be dried and steeped, providing an acceptable substitute for tea. However, objectionable alkaloids are extracted if steeped too long.

2/3x Van Bruggen photo

MOSCHATEL

Adoxa moschatellina Moschatel Family June - July

This wildflower is included here, not because it is common, but because of its rarity in the northern plains. It grows on moss-covered rocks in canyons where it is cool and shaded. Although it ranges from Ontario west to Utah, in our area it is found only in the Black Hills. The common name is derived from the musky odor of the tuberous roots. Another common name of the plant is Muskroot. The plants are very small, not more than 5 inches tall, and have three to six tiny, green-white flowers at the top of the stem.

2x Van Bruggen photo

FALSE GROMWELL

Onosmodium molle Borage Family June - July

Native prairie remnants usually have False Gromwell as a frequent inhabitant. Typical of the borage family, this member has sticky hairs on the leaves and flowers in coiled clusters that unroll as they open. Several stems grow from a deep-seated rootstock. At maturity they may be as tall as 2 feet. The white to green, funnel-shaped flowers are about ½ inch long. False Gromwell is common in the northern plains and ranges from Minnesota to New Mexico.

1/2x Van Bruggen photo

GREEN GENTIAN

Swertia radiata Gentian Family June

There are several green gentians in the western United States. This one is found from the Black Hills of South Dakota west to California. A prominent plant, it has a stout, unbranched stem that reaches over 3 feet high. The long, sword-shaped leaves radiate out from the stem in a whorled fashion. The flowers are white to green with purple spots, and each petal face has a pair of glandular areas. It grows in moist areas of open woods and valleys.

1/5x Van Bruggen photo

SEGOLILY

Calochortus gunnisonii Lily Family late May - June

The entire plant is edible; however, it was the bulb that provided food for Indians. It was made the state flower of Utah after being credited for saving the lives of Mormon pioneers when their crops were damaged by crickets. The bulbs, about an inch across, taste much like potato when boiled or baked and are quite nutritious. Flowers are creamy-white with a magenta base. The grasslike leaves are few and roll inward. This perennial herb inhabits hillsides and dry, open areas in the western half of the Dakotas and Nebraska and westward. The name "Sego" is of Shoshone origin.

1x Stockert photo

PALE EVENING-PRIMROSE

Oenothera albicaulis Evening-primrose Family late May - June

There are more than 25 species of evening-primrose that are native to the high plains. This one is a branched annual that grows up to 18 inches tall. Each showy, white flower is up to 4 inches in diameter. They are short-lived, lasting only a day or so. As is typical for cream-colored or white flowers, they open in the evening when their nectaries attract night-flying insects. This herb prefers dry, sandy soil of prairie or sandy washouts of stream beds.

1/2x Stockert photo

LARGEFLOWER TOWNSENDIA

Townsendia grandiflora Aster Family late May - June

This perennial herb grows sparsely in dry prairie or on eroded clay banks. It is inconspicuous except when in bloom. Large in comparison with the rest of the plant, the flower heads display yellow centers surrounded by pinkish-tinged, white ray florets. The 2-inch heads appear singly or in small clusters from the short stems which branch from a substantial root. Indians ate the branched, root crown of this plant and pioneers used its flowers to decorate churches at Easter time.

1x Stockert photo

COMMON YARROW

Achillea millefolium Aster Family late May - August

Millefoium, meaning "thousand leaves," describes the many segments of compound leaves which give this perennial a fern-like appearance before it blooms in clusters of flower heads. This is a naturalized plant from Europe, where, for centuries, it has been used as a medicine. Here it is common in waste places, overgrazed pastures, and along roadsides. The herb, especially the leaves, produces an aromatic volatile oil and was steeped for tea, chewed for toothache, and generally used as a stimulant or tonic. Winnebago Indians wadded the leaves in their ears as a treatment for earaches.

1/2x Van Bruggen photo

SMOOTH SUMAC

Rhus glabra Cashew Family June

A shrubby plant with several stems, Smooth Sumac prefers open hillsides and the edges of woods. The greenish-white flowers grow in dense clusters at the ends of branches. In autumn the leaves turn bright red before falling. The deep red fruits, which remain when other food is snow-covered, provide a plentiful alternate source of winter food for birds. Indians steeped the fruits for tea and pounded the seeds into flour which was made into gruel, a bread-like food. This was not part of their regular diet, but served as survival food during severe winters.

1/3x Van Bruggen photo

MEADOW ANEMONE

Anemone canadensis Buttercup Family June - July

The white sepals on Meadow Anemone look like petals. As in all the anemones, true petals are lacking. Spreading by rhizomes, this perennial frequently inhabits roadside ditches and moist prairie. Hairy stems grow up to 2 feet with leaves deeply and irregularly lobed but oval to round in outline. Small, dry, one-seeded fruits, called achenes, crowd together forming a bristly, spherical head. Medicine men of the Plains Indians made a decoction from the vegetative parts of the herb to wash the wounds of their people. Although rare westward, it is common in the eastern Dakotas and Nebraska, and eastward.

1/3x Van Bruggen photo

INDIAN HEMP

Apocynum cannabinum Dogbane Family June - July

The name Dogbane is derived from a Greek name whose true meaning is lost and perhaps has nothing to do with dogs. The term Indian Hemp does relate to the fact that Indians collected and processed the willowy stems to make articles such as mats and baskets. A perennial, it grows in open soils and thickets over the plains. The white flowers top the stems which reach 3 or more feet high. When broken, the stems yield a milky juice. Indian Hemp is a relative of the milkweeds but has pods that are longer and very narrow.

1/3x Van Bruggen photo

MOUNTAIN BALM

Ceanothus velutinus Buckthorn Family June - July

A number of common names have been applied to this member of the **Ceanothus** group, but Mountain Balm is perhaps the most used. A large shrub, it is found at middle altitudes in the Rocky Mountains and at upper altitudes in the Black Hills. The leaves are thick and evergreen, that is, they do not drop off in the fall. They serve as valuable winter browse for deer and elk. The white flowers are produced in dense, upright clusters. Note the similarity to Inland Ceanothus (see page 56). Many small ovoid fruits are formed after flowering.

1/2x Van Bruggen photo

PALE DOGWOOD

Cornus amomum Dogwood Family June - July

This shrub is not the most common member of the dogwood family in the central and northern plains. That distinction belongs to the closely related species, Red Osier, which has flowers and leaves very similar to the one illustrated, but possesses prominently reddish branches. The shrubby dogwoods are densely branched and reach 10 feet tall. They are important as understory shrubs in woodlands and are common along waterways. Their fruits are berry-like and provide valuable winter feed for wildlife.

3/4x Van Bruggen photo

PLAINS LARKSPUR

Delphinium carolinianum Buttercup Family June - July

The native habitat for this prairie perennial extends westward from Iowa to the foothills of the Rocky Mountains. The dissected, crowfoot-like leaves contain an alkaloid called delphinine, which is poisonous to grazing animals. The flowers, up to 1½ inches long, are arranged along the main stem. They are adapted for receiving night-flying moths who act as pollinators. One sepal of the flower has a modified base forming an upward projecting spur which contains nectar. When in bloom, the herbs are conspicuous in dry areas of the high plains where they may grow to more than 30 inches tall.

1x Van Bruggen photo

SCARLET ELDERBERRY

Sambucus racemosa Honeysuckle Family June - July

These large shrubs, 5 to 10 feet tall, usually grow in thickets and are particularly noticeable in the Black Hills. Small, white flowers form branched, dense clusters called cymes. Each cyme is 2 to 8 inches across. The profuse, red to purple berries ripen in July and August and are bitter to the taste because of the presence of saponin, a soapy-like material. Wildlife carefully avoid eating them. A closely related species, the American, or Common, Elderberry (*S. canadensis*), is frequent eastward. Its berries are a deeper purple and are edible.

1/2x Kravig photo

OX-EYE DAISY

Chrysanthemum leucanthemum Aster Family June - August

This herb is a native of Eurasia and has become naturalized throughout most of temperate North America. It is frequently seen along roadsides, in disturbed prairie, and on railroad embankments. A perennial, it spreads underground by a rhizome, an elongated bulb-like root system. Stems grow up to 2 feet with solitary flower heads. The outer, white ray florets account for the name *leucanthemum*, which means "white flower." Ox-eye Daisy transplants to gardens very successfully; in fact, it may take over a garden!

2/3x Van Bruggen photo

BLUESTEM PRICKLYPOPPY

Argemone polyanthemos Poppy Family June - September

Large flowers up to 4 inches across characterize this more or less prickly plant. The blossoms, each with six papery petals, are followed by spiny-edged fruits that are about an inch long. Its leaves are silvery blue and also have a spiny edge. A sticky, yellow juice oozes out when the stems are broken. Animals carefully avoid this annual herb because of its spines and un-palatable juices. The plant grows up to 3 feet or more and is particularly common in the sand-hills of Nebraska, although it is seen in other parts of that state and in South Dakota.

1x Stockert photo

CATNIP

Nepeta cataria Mint Family June - September

This flower is an excellent example of specialization for insect pollination. Each blossom is about ½ inch long, with an open throat that welcomes each insect visitor. The flowers are arranged in spikes at the ends of branched stems that grow 2 to 4 feet tall. The arrow-shaped leaves with rounded "teeth" are softly hairy and aromatic. The minty aroma of the herb does attract cats who enjoy rolling in it. Old manuals of medicine recommended extracts of Catnip for curing colic in infants. A native of Europe, Catnip has become a perennial resident throughout the United States.

3/4x Van Bruggen photo

WESTERN SNOWBERRY

Symphoricarpos occidentalis Honeysuckle Family mid June - August

The white fruits of this shrub are easier to see than the white to pink flowers which bloom in dense clusters. Two-foot-tall Western Snowberry favors open hillsides and replaces prairie grasses that are overgrazed by livestock. Dakota Indians used the stems and roots as a survival food and the fruits as a laxative. They also pounded the roots and steeped them to make a medicine for treating colds. Small amounts of saponin-like alkaloids are present in the leaves.

3x Stockert photo

RATTLEBOX

Crotalaria sagittalis Legume Family July - September

The small, pale yellow flowers of Rattlebox quickly fade to white and are mostly covered by the green floral leaves. The more obvious structure is the large, green inflated pod on the elongated flower stalk shown here. Rattlebox is an annual with stems branched, growing to 12 inches or more. The leaves are lance-shaped, erect and about one and a half inches long. After the flowers mature, the resulting green fruit enlarges, turns black, and encloses 2 or more shiny brown seeds that become loose. When shaken, the seeds rattle in the pod. Rattlebox may be locally common on rocky slopes, sandy areas, and sand dunes in the eastern part of the northern plains.

1/3x Van Bruggen photo

BRACTED ORCHID

Habenaria viridis Orchid Family June - July

This orchid is quite common and is easily recognized by the long, green bracts beneath the flowers. Unlike most orchids, it is not very showy. The flowers are mostly green with some white color on the lips. The lip has two or three teeth or indentations, a distinguishing characteristic not found on the Northern Green Orchid (see page 29). Stems are unbranched and up to 2 feet tall, with several ovate to lance-shaped leaves. The Bracted Orchid grows in damp woods throughout the northern plains, including the Black Hills. There are ten species of **Habenaria** orchids in this region.

2/3x Van Bruggen photo

HIGHBUSH CRANBERRY

Viburnum opulus Honeysuckle Family June - July

A native of moist woods in the northern part of the United States and into Canada, Highbush Cranberry is a woody shrub that often reaches 6 feet or more. The dark green leaves have three prominent lobes. Flowers are rounded or flat topped inflorescences called cymes. Often the marginal flowers are sterile with large petals. The small, red fruits are similar to cranberries. A number of the **Viburnum** species are cultivated and commonly called Snowball Shrubs. In our region Highbush Cranberry ranges from eastern North Dakota to the Black Hills.

1/2x Van Bruggen photo

WHITE PRAIRIECLOVER

Petalostemum candidum Legume Family mid June - September

This legume is important for its forage value to grazing animals. It has small flowers arranged in a dense spike up to 2 inches long. Flowering starts at the base and moves up to the tip. Plants are perennial from woody roots. Stems branch primarily from the base and grow to a height of 2 feet or more. The compound leaves are divided into narrow, linear leaflets. Indian women collected many plants which they tied together to make crude brooms for sweeping the lodge. Widespread in the plains, this herb is native from Minnesota to Arizona.

1x Van Bruggen photo

SNOW-ON-THE-MOUNTAIN

Euphorbia marginata Spurge Family mid June - September

This showy annual inhabits dry hillsides and prairies. The upper leaves immediately below the small, inconspicuous flower clusters have prominently whitened margins which, when seen from a distance, cause dense patches of this herb to give a whitish appearance; hence, its common name. Native from Minnesota to Montana and south, it is widely cultivated elsewhere. The stems of most species of **Euphorbia** have an acrid latex that is irritating to skin and to linings of intestinal tracts. Several other alkaloids, not completely understood, are also present. None appear to have any beneficial value.

1x Stockert photo

BUNCHBERRY

Cornus canadensis Dogwood Family late June - July

Most members of the Dogwood Family are trees or shrubs, but this species is a small herb which springs from an extensive, bulb-like root system, or rhizome. Stems grow up to 10 inches or more with four to six leaves forming a circle around each stem. The flowers are in a small cluster with four whitened leaves beneath that serve to attract the insects in the same way as petals. Later, scarlet fruits attract birds and mammals. Ranging from Greenland to California, this perennial herb occurs in the Black Hills and in the Turtle Mountains.

2/3x Kravig photo

DUCKPOTATO ARROWHEAD

Sagittaria cuneata Waterplantain Family late June - September

The tuberous, underground parts of this herbaceous perennial and other arrowheads were eaten by many North American Indians. The tubers provided a welcome change in diet after a long winter when ice and frozen earth prevented getting most other plant foods. When cooked, they taste similar to Irish potatoes. The sexes of the flowers are separate; the lower ones are female; the upper, male. This photograph shows only male flowers. Arrowheads grow in shallow water, in potholes, and at the margin of lakes and slow streams. Waterfowl, especially diving ducks, feed extensively on the young shoots and tubers.

1x Stockert photo

COMMON PEARLY-EVERLASTING

Anaphalis margaritacea Aster Family July - August

A conspicuous plant of dry, open prairie and rocky slopes, this perennial grows up to 2 feet or higher, with linear (long and narrow) leaves that may be more than 4 inches long. The leaves and flowers are wooly-white for most of the growing season, giving rise to the common name. The flower head has many dense, pearly-white bracts. After flowering, whitened hairs aid in seed dispersal. This herb is quite common in the Black Hills.

1/3x Kravig photo

CULVERS-ROOT

Veronicastrum virginicum Snapdragon Family July - August

The sometimes lavender-tinged blossoms of this perennial have projecting, needle-like stamens. The flowers cluster into a long, tapering, distinctive spike. Stems grow up to 6 feet, bearing leaves in whorls, or circles, with 3 to 6 in a whorl. The juices contain a strong emetic and laxative, and were used as medicine. This herb prefers moist places in prairie and thickets. Although present from the eastern half of the Dakotas and Nebraska eastward, it is rare in the central and western parts of the northern plains. The origin of the common name is unknown.

1/3x Van Bruggen photo

65

COW PARSNIP

Heracleum sphondylium Parsley Family July

A large, perennial weed, this plant is often found in marshy or rich, damp soil. The name Cow Parsnip refers to the coarse and rough appearance of the stems and leaves. It grows to 6 feet tall. The stem is stout and has a heavy, branched root system. The flowers are arranged in large, umbelled clusters, which are characteristic of the family. After flowering, the fruits remain on the branches for several months. They are flat and heart-shaped with several ribs and oil tubes lining each face. Cow Parsnip is common over the northern plains.

1/7x Van Bruggen photo

MOUNTAIN MEADOWSWEET

Spiraea betulifolia Rose Family June - July

Two meadowsweets are found in the northern plains. This one is not as common as the other, *S. alba*, which grows in open meadows and moist prairies. Mountain Meadowsweet is found, as the name implies, in mountainous areas of the Black Hills and west in the Rocky Mountains as far as British Columbia. A small shrub, it was woody stems that are often less than 2 feet tall. The small, white flowers are in dense clusters at the tops of the stems. The nectar is very sweet-smelling and attracts hosts of insects. The term *Spiraea* comes from the ancient Greek word for wreath, hence the term Bridal Wreath for the commonly cultivated form.

1x Van Bruggen photo

BALLHEAD ERIOGONUM

Eriogonum pauciflorum Buckwheat Family July

Of the dozen or more *Eriogonums* found in the Great Plains, this and the Bracted Umbrella Plant (page 31), are among the ones most commonly encountered. A drab, gray-appearing plant, it has stems that are short and form dense mats with most of the leaves at the soil level. The flowering stalks are almost leafless. Clusters of very small, white-pink flowers develop in mid-summer. The deep root system of the plant allows it to grow in such inhospitable places as dry, sandy knolls and clay flats such as are found in the Badlands.

2/3x Van Bruggen photo

BROAD-LIPPED TWAYBLADE

Listera convallarioides Orchid Family July - August

The pair of roundish, broad leaves about midway on the stem of this perennial orchid account for the common name. Intricate flowers, usually yellowish-green, are arranged in a loose, spike-like fashion. Plants occasionally have stems taller than 1 foot. The herb grows in damp humus of rich woods from New England to the Midwest, but is restricted to the Black Hills in the northern plains area. All orchids should be seen and appreciated in their native habitat, not picked or transplanted!

1/2x Kravig photo

WHITE CAMPION

Lychnis alba Pink Family July - August

The flowers of White Campion, or White Cockle, bloom at night when night-flying moths serve as the principal pollinators. The male and female flowers are on separate plants; those pictured here are female. The notched petals radiate above an enlarged calyx, the whorl of leaves, or sepals, at the base of the flower. The female flowers mature into capsules with a toothed opening. A great number of small seeds are produced. A frequent perennial, possibly biennial, of roadsides and waste places, this herb grows up to 3 feet. Its range is widespread in the eastern United States.

1/2x Van Bruggen photo

BOUNCING-BET

Saponaria officinalis Pink Family July - September

When Bouncing-bet escapes from cultivation, it becomes a persisting perennial of roadsides and waste places, spreading by its roots. The herbs grow up to 2 feet or more with strictly opposite leaves. The pinkish-white flowers are borne in dense clusters on the stem at points where leaves branch off and at the top of the stem. Typical of the Pink Family, the petals are notched or lobed. The generic name, *Saponaria*, refers to the soapy material, saponin, which is in the stems. Although saponin is poisonous, animals avoid it because it is extremely distasteful.

1/2x Van Bruggen photo

WHORLED MILKWEED

Asclepias verticillata Milkweed Family July - September

The white flowers of this herb are smaller than those of other milkweeds. The normally unbranched stem, up to 2 feet tall, contains a milky juice which is poisonous to livestock. The linear leaves are verticillate, or whorled, which means that several leaves radiate from a point on the stem. Each leaf is 1 to 3 inches long. A perennial, it grows in patches from spreading underground parts. This milkweed is widely distributed on the plains.

2x Stockert photo

WESTERN FALSE-BONESET

Kuhnia eupatorioides Aster Family July - October

The words **eupatorioides** and "boneset" indicate that there is some similarity to *Eupatorium*, the Joe-pye-weeds or true bonesets (see page 94). This likeness is seen in the structure of the flower heads which consist only of tubular florets. The heads of Western False-boneset are made up of about 30 white to yellow florets. The herb grows to 3 feet or taller with several upright branches off the main stem. Leaves are alternate, not opposite, as in the true bonesets. Ranging from the East Coast to the Rockies and south to Arizona, this perennial inhabits prairies and other dry, open places.

1x Stockert photo

WHITE PRAIRIE ASTER

Aster falcatus Aster Family late July - October

Ranging from the Pacific northwest to Nebraska and the western Dakotas, this perennial is a common inhabitant of dry prairies. It is recognized by its flower heads that cluster at the ends and sides of branches. Each head is about ½ inch across. Sometimes the ray florets are pink. The leaves are oblong and about ¾ of an inch long. The herb seldom grows more than 2 feet high.

2x Stockert photo

FIELD MINT

Mentha arvensis Mint Family July - August

Although grouped in the white flower section, the flowers of the Common or Field Mint often vary to rosy-pink. The very small flowers are sessile, that is, without stalks, and crowded in the leaf axils in such a way as to appear to encircle the stem. The leaves have a strong, minty odor. Field Mint is very common in moist or marshy places ranging from Newfoundland to Alaska. The well known plants Spearmint and Peppermint are also in the genus **Mentha**. They are found throughout the United States and Europe. For centuries they have been cultivated for their essential oils which are used for flavoring. Indians used the Field Mint for flavoring, and they steeped a tea from the leaves and flowers.

3/4x Van Bruggen photo

SMARTWEED

Polygonum pennsylvanicum Buckwheat Family August

The Smartweeds are very common in the plains. At least 25 species occur in the northern plains. This one is an ever-present weed in fields and waste places. An annual, the branched stems often grow to a height of 4 feet. Flowers often are pink, fading to white as they age. The leaves are lance-shaped and about 5 inches long. Each plant produces many seeds each year. Not all germinate the following year; some remaining dormant for several years. The Smartweeds are well known by farmers who are serious in their weed control efforts.

1/4x Van Bruggen photo

THIMBLEBERRY

Rubus parviflorus Rose Family July - August

A relative of the raspberries and blackberries, this attractive, shrubby woodland inhabitant is found on slopes at high altitudes in the Black Hills. It ranges in distribution from Ontario to southern Alaska. Plants are irregularly branched and several feet tall. The leaves are broadly 3- or 5-lobed; often up to 10 inches across. The white flowers are about 2 inches across and very showy. Later in the season, red, raspberry-like fruits are formed which are ½ - ¾ of an inch in diameter. They taste a little soapy and are not particularly relished by wildlife.

1/3x Van Bruggen photo

BICKNELL GERANIUM

Geranium bicknellii Geranium Family August

Typical of the half dozen or so geranium species of the area, this annual or biennial has the characteristic five petals in a symmetrical pattern around a common center. The flowers usually form in pairs in hues from light pink to purple marked with reddish streaks. After flowering, the maturing fruit becomes extended with a beak, hence the use of Cranesbill as another common name. The leaves of the herb are circular in outline with deep incisions. Found in woodlands and thickets, it is also present in the Turtle Mountains of North Dakota and in the Black Hills.

2x Van Bruggen photo

WHITESTEM EVENING-PRIMROSE

Oenothera nuttallii Evening-primrose Family August - September

This perennial has white stems that are so smooth they look as if they were enameled. The flowers are at first white but soon become pink or rose. Each one is about 2 inches across. Plants grow to a height of 2 feet, often branching at the upper part of the main stem. Leaves are oblong and lack the obvious "teeth" so common in other closely related species. The herb spreads by creeping roots in open, flat areas of prairie and can form large, dense patches.

1x Stockert photo

NODDING LADIES-TRESSES

Spiranthes vernalis Orchid Family early September

The nodding, greenish-white flowers of this orchid appear to form a spiral, but close examination reveals that they grow in three rows on a slightly twisted stalk, thus giving the appearance of a spiral. Flower stalks are 20 to 40 inches tall. Two to four stems sprout from a perennial bulb-like root, or rhizome. The leaves are narrow and grow mostly at the base. Growing in bogs or open marshy places in the eastern high plains, this striking rare native herb should be conserved wherever found!

2/3x Van Bruggen photo

SPRING CRESS

Cardamine bulbosa Mustard Family April - June

The scientific name **Cardamine** is from the Greek meaning cress. The species name **bulbosa** refers to the deep-seated bulbous or tuberous base. Spring Cress is a perennial with a simple or rarely branched stem 10 or more inches tall. It is one of the earlier spring flowers in marshes or creek bottoms in the eastern part of the Northern Plains. The white flowers with 4 oppositely arranged petals, typical of the Mustard family, later form elongate pods one to one and a half inches long. Native Americans and early settlers collected the plants for use as a tangy condiment for food in early spring after a long, dreary winter of dried or salted food.

1/2x Van Bruggen photo

WHITE-EYED GRASS

Sisyrinchium campestre Iris Family May - June

White-eyed Grass isn't always as white as this picture. Flowers may be pale blue, or, as the white petals mature, they may turn a pale blue. The small white-eyed grass is a welcome bit of color in the meadows of the Northern Plains in early spring. The stems, from 5 to 10 inches tall, are narrowly winged and grass-like and grow from a perennial, stringy rhizome in the prairie turf. Small clusters of flowers, in very thin stalks, develop from between a two-valved spathe or bract at the upper part of the stem. Closely related to the Blue-eyed Grass, (see page 98), this species tends to be more common in the eastern parts of our region.

1/3x Van Bruggen photo

DOGTOOTH VIOLET

Erythronium albidum Lily Family April - May

It is unfortunate that the common name of this early spring wildflower is called a violet. It really is like a miniature lily. The word dogtooth refers to the small white bulb deep in the ground from which the 1 or 2 leaves and a single flowering stalk grows. Dogtooth violets grow in large perennial patches at the edges of woods in the eastern part of the Northern Plains. Older bulbs send out underground branches which form new bulbs. Flowering stalks are 4 to 8 inches tall with a recurved tip from which a single, pendant flower appears. As is the case with most lilies, the 6 perianth parts, consisting of 3 petals and 3 sepals, are similar in shape and color and sharply bend back, revealing the 6 yellow anthers.

1/3x Van Bruggen photo

WHITE LADY SLIPPER

Cypripedium candidum Orchid Family May - June

This beautiful orchid is becoming very rare in the Northern Plains. However, this picture was taken in late May in the wet meadow of a protected wildlife refuge where there were over two hundred plants. It was a rare sight! The slipper or lip of White Lady Slipper is nearly one inch long with pale rose veins. The other perianth parts are green to brown with lavender veins. Usually only one flower is produced on each stem. Plants are 8 to 12 inches tall with 3 to 5 broad, green leaves. When these orchids are found, they should never be moved in hope of saving them. Instead, the habitat where they are located should be saved.

1/6x Van Bruggen photo

ONE-FLOWERED WINTERGREEN

Pyrola uniflora Wintergreen Family June - July

This delicate little plant grows in mossy, shaded woods in the cooler parts of the Black Hills. It ranges across North America in similar wooded areas. The solitary stem, from 4 to 6 inches tall, has at its recurved tip a single, greenish-white flower. It is two-thirds of an inch across with a fragrant odor that attracts insects for pollination. The several basal leaves are evergreen, their blades less than one inch across. After flowering, a single rounded fruit, about one-fourth of an inch in diameter develops, producing many seeds.

2x Van Bruggen photo

WHITE SHINLEAF

Pyrola elliptica Wintergreen Family July

Because this plant is found in drier upland woods than any other of the **Pyrola** group, it is probably the one that is most commonly found in the Black Hills. The solitary stem grows to 10 inches tall and has 8 to 12 white flowers on short, recurved stalks around the stem. The flowers are fragrant, about three-fourths of an inch across, with 5 spreading petals. The 3 to 7 leaves are mostly basal, elliptic in shape, and evergreen.

1/3x Van Bruggen photo

WHITE CAMASS

Zigadenus elegans Lily Family June - July

This species of Camass, like the Grassy Deathcamass on page 52, is poisonous. White Camass is a robust plant up to 2 feet tall, with grassy-like leaves and a large, branched flower cluster called an open raceme. There may be more than 25 flowers on each plant. The flowers are six-parted, greenish-white, about three-fourths of an inch across. Like many plants in the Lily Family, it grows from a deep-seated fibrous-coated bulb that may be mistaken for a wild onion. This relatively common moist prairie native is found in the eastern part of the Northern Plains whereas the Grassy Deathcamass is more western in its distribution.

1/5x Van Bruggen photo

WHITE MILKWORT

Polygala alba Milkwort Family June - July

White milkwort is a perennial from a stout, vertical root. The stems are usually simple or sparingly branched, up to 12 or 14 inches tall. Its leaves are small and linear. A prominent feature is the compact, tapered cluster of white flowers, each about one-half inch long. Grazing animals avoid the milkwort because of its bitter taste. White Milkwort is the most common of the 5 or 6 milkworts in the Great Plains, occurring on dry prairies and sandy slopes.

1/2x Van Bruggen photo

WATER HYSSOP

Bacopa rotundifolia Snapdragon Family July - August

The leaves of the Water Hyssop are characteristically shiny-smooth, rounded in outline, and without stalks. Plants are rooted in mud of shallow water with the stems floating to the surface. They also may persist as prostrate plants in muddy areas. Flowers are white with a yellow throat, the petals about one-half inch long. This plant occurs throughout the northern plains in springs and ponds. It is spread by migrating waterfowl that eat or otherwise carry seeds from one place to another. Other species of Water Hyssop are common in the tropics.

1x Van Bruggen photo

AMERICAN BUGLEWEED

Lycopus americanus Mint Family June - August

Most members of this family have a minty odor when vegetative parts are crushed. However, the several Bugleweeds in our region belonging to the genus *Lycopus* are exceptions, not having this characteristic. Plants are perennial from a spreading rootstock, the several simple stems about 12 to 18 inches tall. Its leaves are opposite each other on the squarish stem and deeply incised. Up to 20 white flowers are produced in a dense mass around the stem at the points of attachment of the leaves. They are small, each less than one-fourth of an inch long. American Bugleweed is common in marshy or aquatic areas over the northern plains.

1/3x Van Bruggen photo

DWARF BLACKBERRY

Rubus pubescens Rose Family June - July

The Dwarf Blackberry is also known as Creeping Blackberry because of its weak, trailing stems. The Blackberries and Raspberries are a complex group and have been the object of much study by plant classifiers. This species, however, is quite distinct. It is without thorns or bristles on the stems and the leaves are compound with 3 leaflets, somewhat like the strawberries. One to 3 white flowers form at the ends of stems, each about one-half inch across. The fruits are red to purple, also about one-half inch, raspberry-like and sharp-tasting. Dwarf Blackberry can be found in moist and rocky woods throughout the Black Hills.

1/2x Van Bruggen photo

WHITE SNAKEROOT

Eupatorium rugosum Aster Family July - September

White Snakeroot is a woodland plant that occurs in the eastern part of the Great Plains. A perennial, the stems may be over 3 feet tall. Leaves are broadly ovate, opposite, and dark green. In late summer it produces many small, white flowerheads, each less than one-half inch across. This plant is poisonous to animals. Dairy cattle who graze on it become ill with "trembles." The soluble poison, tremetol, imparted to milk, may be transmitted to humans who drink it, giving symptoms called "milk sickness."

1/4x Van Bruggen photo

SWAMP LOUSEWORT

Pedicularis lanceolata Snapdragon Family August - September

This lousewort is closely related to the Common Lousewort, page 24, which grows in drier prairies and is much smaller in stature. The swamp lousewort has simple to branched stems one and a half feet tall, and the flower cluster is not as compact. The flowers are pale yellow to nearly white, with petals up to one inch long. This picture was taken early when the flowers were forming. Later the upper flower stalks elongate, forming a more elongate cluster. The common name lousewort was from an old belief that animals who grazed on this plant would become infested with lice. Swamp lousewort is found in wet places in the eastern part of the Great Plains.

1/4x Van Bruggen photo

ENCHANTER'S NIGHTSHADE

Circaea alpina Evening-primrose Family July - August

This delicate little perennial is at home in circumboreal (around the North Pole) woods from Labrador to Alaska. It has stems 4 to 6 inches tall, and 4 to 6 broadly ovate leaves which are light green. The tiny white flowers are on slender stalks and open before the main flowering stalk elongates. There are but 2 small white petals on each flower. The fruit is a small, teardrop shaped structure covered with hooked bristles. In the Black Hills this species hybridizes with our other more common species **Circaea lutetiana**, producing sterile hybrids. Enchanter's Nightshade may be found in shady, moist ravines and on moss-covered rocks or logs.

2/3x Van Bruggen photo

FOXTAIL DALEA

Dalea leporina Legume Family August - September

There are over a dozen Daleas in the Great Plains. All are similar in the respect that their flowers are in compact, terminal clusters called spikes or racemes (See the Silktop Dalea, page 30). The Foxtail Dalea is an annual and grows in low, sandy areas, disturbed edges of fields, and along stream banks. The stems are branched, up to 18 inches tall, with leaves having up to 24 pairs of small leaflets. Flowers are white to pale blue, less than one-half inch long, with many small, erect purple hairs beneath each flower, giving the cluster a lavender color. Livestock will graze on this plant when it is abundant.

1x Van Bruggen photo

SPREADING PASQUEFLOWER

Anemone patens Buttercup Family late March - May

The state flower of South Dakota and one of the earliest on the prairie, Spreading Pasqueflower blooms before surrounding vegetation turns green. The outer parts of the flower, which look like petals, are actually sepals and vary from white to deep lavender. Although the color variance may be caused partly by genetic influences, it is primarily thought to be the result of variable life processes. The long, feathery-tipped fruits suggest the name Prairie-smoke, by which this herbaceous perennial is also called. Spreading Pasqueflower grows throughout the high plains.

1/2x Stockert photo

Red Flowers

MOUNTAIN WAFER-PARSNIP

Cymopterus montanus Parsley Family April - May

One of several wafer-parsnips, or wild parsleys, of the prairie, this herb has a perennial taproot and deeply-cut leaves. The very small, white to purplish flowers form dense umbels, an arrangement which produces a flat to rounded, attractive landing site for insect pollinators. Prairie Indians roasted the roots, then ground them into meal which was baked or made into a thin porridge. It is a common resident on rocky slopes of the Black Hills and the surrounding plains.

1/2x Stockert photo

MISSOURI MILKVETCH

Astragalus missouriensis Legume Family mid April - June

Of the more than 50 species of **Astragalus** that inhabit North America, Missouri Milkvetch is one of the most common. It is characterized by low stems about 4 inches long. The leaflets appear silvery gray due to dense, flattened hairs on the surface. The fruits mature as fleshy pods 3 inches long. Prairie Indians collected various kinds of milkvetch pods for use in soups and other cooking. This perennial herb frequents hills and prairies throughout the northern plains.

1x Stockert photo

DAMES ROCKET

Hesperis matronalis Mustard Family mid April - June

The name *Hesperis*, or "Vesper-flower," was given to this plant over 2,000 years ago, for it gives out a lovely perfume only in the evening. The herb was cultivated in Roman gardens by matrons because of its fragrance. Well established in the eastern United States, it persists after cultivation along roadsides and in old gardens in the eastern part of the northern plains. Stems grow from 6 inches to 4 feet tall or more, depending upon available moisture. The flowers are usually deep lavender but may vary to a lighter color. A biennial, it blooms during its second year.

1/3x Van Bruggen photo

CANADA WILDGINGER

Asarum canadense Birthwort Family late April - May

Lacking petals, the flower of this woodland plant has, instead, three brownish-purple sepals which form the showy parts. The flower is borne at the level of the forest litter near the base of the usually paired, heart-shaped leaves. The inside of the flower usually harbors insects which quite accidentally aid in pollination. A common, perennial herb of eastern forests, it occurs infrequently on the loamy slopes of rich woods at the eastern edge of the plains. The horizontal roots, up to ½ inch in diameter, have a ginger-like odor, hence the common name.

1/2x Van Bruggen photo

PRAIRIE VIOLET

Viola pedatifida Violet Family May - June

The most common violet of the high plains, this low perennial is essentially stemless and grows less than 6 inches high. The deeply divided leaves and large, blue to purple flowers distinguish the herb from other blue violets. In all native violets, one of the five petals has a sac-like base which is called a spur. Three of the petals have hairs or beards on the inner surfaces. Several violets, including this one, hybridize freely with other closely related species, making identification of their offspring impossible.

1x Van Bruggen photo

PURPLESPOT FRITILLARY

Fritillaria atropurpurea Lily Family May - June

The spotted flowers of this perennial account for another common name, Leopard Lily. The drooping blossoms are a dull purplish-brown and somewhat ill-smelling; however, they attract insect pollinators. The lily-like stems grow up to 2 feet, bearing long, narrow leaves aligned alternately. Absent in eastern North and South Dakota, the herb becomes more frequent westward in the drier prairies. Indians called it Rice Root because the offshoots and the scales of the bulb resemble grains of rice. The bulbs are starchy and good to eat.

1x Stockert photo

SOUTHERN SHOOTINGSTAR

Dodecatheon pulchellum Primrose Family May - June

There are more than 15 species of shootingstar in temperate North America, ranging from Alaska to Georgia. This herbaceous perennial is considered to be cordilleran, meaning "of the mountains," and occurs in the Black Hills in marshy soil along streams. Scapes, or leafless stalks, from 6 to 12 inches high, bear pink to purple flowers. The 5 petals flare back and the conspicuous, reddish tips of the stamens form a tight cone which points downward. The flat, spoon-shaped leaves grow in a rosette at the base of the plant.

1/2x Kravig photo

LAMBERT CRAZYWEED

Oxytropis lambertii Legume Family May - June

One of a group of plants called locoweeds, this stemless herb is toxic to all grazing animals if enough is eaten. The compound leaves and flowering scapes, or leafless stalks, arise from a thick crown at ground level. This is a good way to distinguish it from **Astragulus** (see pages 56 and 76), a related genus with which it is often confused. **Astragalus** has leafy stems with flowers at the tops. Flowers of Lambert Crazyweed are deep purple but may lighten as the sun bleaches them. This perennial is one of several species of **Oxytropis** that are native to the Great Plains.

1/3x Stockert photo

STRIPED CORALROOT

Corallorhiza striata Orchid Family June

Like all of the coralroots, this one is dependent on the dead remains of other plants and fungi in the soil for its nutrition. Its roots are perennial, and from them several stems grow to about 15 inches tall. It forms small, sometimes dense patches under pines at higher altitudes in the Black Hills and also in northern North Dakota in our region. Its distribution in North America ranges from Quebec to British Columbia and southward. Prominent purple stripes on rose-pink flower parts make this a striking wildflower.

1x Van Bruggen photo

POINTED PHLOX

Phlox alyssifolia Phlox Family May - June

Because of its small size and unusually showy flowers, this wildflower is particularly noticed by those who take a close look at the prairie in the Great Plains during May. A perennial, this phlox has a short stem with fibrous, peeling bark. A second characteristic that distinguishes this prairie native is the sharp, pointed leaves with whitened margins. White to rose colored flowers are usually solitary. Each petal is about ½ inch long. It grows from western South Dakota and Nebraska to the Rocky Mountains.

1½ x Van Bruggen photo

BUFFALOBERRY

Shepherdia argentea Oleaster Family May - June

Although May through June is the time of flowering, this picture was taken in late July when the Buffaloberry was in full fruit. The reason that the fruit is pictured is because this is the only time many people notice this shrub. The flowers are very small and dull brown. A perennial shrub, it has bright green leaves. The stems are 4 to 6 feet tall and become thorny after a year or so. Buffaloberries were used by Indians as food throughout the Great Plains. People still collect them for making jams and jellies.

3/4x Van Bruggen photo

SHOWY PEAVINE

Lathyrus polymorphus Legume Family May - June

Showy Peavine grows 6 to 12 inches tall on weak, straggly stems that have tendrils, the threadlike extensions which help support climbing plants. Four to eight pairs of narrow leaflets make up each compound leaf; their texture varies from smooth to densely hairy. The blue to purplish-red flowers are over 1 inch long. Native to dry, sandy plains of Nebraska, Wyoming, and South Dakota, the perennial herb is principally known for its toxic effect on grazing animals. A disease called lathyrism results when excessive amounts are eaten. Symptoms include a partial paralysis of the limbs.

1/2x Stockert photo

VIOLET WOODSORREL

Oxalis violacea Woodsorrel Family May - June

Widespread in the upland prairie, this inconspicuous herb is often overlooked. A small, stemless perennial, it grows from a deep-seated, brown, scaly bulb about ½ inch in diameter. The leaves have three, heart-shaped segments, typical of the Woodsorrel Family. Flowers, each about ¾ inch across, are on naked stems that are 3 to 5 inches high. *Oxalis* comes from the Greek, making "sharp" or "bitter," which is the taste of the oxalic acid in the soft, fleshy vegetative parts. Indian children ate the bulbs, giving it the name *Skidadihorit* which means "sour-like-salt."

1x Van Bruggen photo

SCARLET GAURA

Gaura coccinea Evening-primrose Family May - August

These perennials grow up to 18 inches from deep, spreading roots. Leaves are lanceolate to oblong with toothed edges. The narrow flower clusters may be as long as 10 inches. The pink to scarlet, strap-like flower parts resemble honeysuckle blossoms. A covering of white hairs gives this herb a gray appearance, leaving it quite inconspicuous in the dry plains where it is a typical resident.

3x Stockert photo

BEARBERRY

Arctostaphylos uva-ursi Heath Family late May - June

Bearberry, ranging from California to Labrador, is a low, spreading, woody-stemmed perennial with small, oval leaves. As is true with many members of the Heath Family, it is an evergreen. Single plants form a mat several feet across. The flowers, resembling small urns, are about ½ inch wide. The bright red, pea-sized berries need almost a year to mature and, while not palatable to humans, are reportedly relished by bears. Indians dried the leaves for smoking. Bearberry, also called Kinnikinnick, is common in the Black Hills and in the Turtle Mountains and badlands of North Dakota.

3/4x Kravig photo

SHELL-LEAF PENSTEMON

Penstemon grandiflorus Snapdragon Family late May - June

Many people of the Great Plains insist that this is the showiest and most graceful of all prairie plants. The stems and leaves are smooth and waxy. Stout, unbranched stems grow up to 3 feet, bearing shell-like leaves which are sessile (without stalks). The pale lavender to lilac flowers are 2 inches long or longer. Prairie Indians prepared extracts of the stems and roots of this perennial herb to use for treating fevers and toothaches. Usually found on relatively undisturbed prairie, it can be successfully transplanted to gardens.

1/2x Stockert photo

MEADOW ROSE

Rosa blanda Rose Family late May - June

The several wild roses in the high plains are hard to tell apart. At times they crossbreed and produce hybrids as intermediate forms. Growing up to 30 inches, the stems of this shrub are basically unarmed, having only a few prickles on new wood. The fragrant blossoms are usually pink, but may vary from white to deep red. Fruits are called rose hips and become valuable winter food for wildlife. An inhabitant of prairie or prairie remnants along roads, the wild rose is the state flower of Iowa and North Dakota.

1/3x Van Bruggen photo

BRACTED SPIDERWORT

Tradescantia bracteata Spiderwort Family late May - July

The flowers of this midwestern native vary from pale pink to deep purple or blue. This color variation may result from the acidity or alkalinity of the soil and from genetic differences in the plants. The short-lived flowers usually close during the heat of the day and re-open before morning. Growing 1 to 2 feet tall with grassy leaves, this herb prefers moist habitats such as roadside ditches, railroad embankments, and other open places. Prairie Indians used the succulent stems as potherbs. This perennial transplants to gardens very successfully.

2x Stockert photo

SCARLET GLOBEMALLOW

Sphaeralcea coccinea Mallow Family late May - September

This common, showy perennial of sandy, high prairie soil spreads from creeping roots. The nearly foot-tall stems bear leaves that are divided into narrow segments, much like those of its "cousin," Flower-of-an-hour (see page 37). Branched, grayish hairs, visible only through a hand lens, cover the vegetative parts. Creamy-yellow, central stamen columns vividly accent the brick-red blossoms. Plains Indians chewed the mucilages and gums in the stems; they also valued the herb as a medicine.

1x Stockert photo

DOWNY PHLOX

Phlox pilosa Phlox Family June - July

Downy, or Prairie Phlox, has soft hairs on the stems. The plants are perennial and grow 1 to 2 feet tall with opposite, lance-shaped leaves. The flowers, which are densely clustered at the ends of branches, are generally in hues from pink to lavender. The blossoms are tubular below and flare into five limbs above to a diameter of about an inch. Growing in low or moist prairie, this herb is found only in the eastern part of the northern plains where it is relatively common. Several garden varieties were adapted from this and other closely related species.

1/2x Van Bruggen photo

HOUNDS-TONGUE

Cynoglossum officinale Borage Family June - July

The common name of this weed of the Great Plains is a translation of the word **Cynoglossum**, meaning "dog" and "tongue." It refers to the leaves, which are rough and shaped like a tongue. Plants are biennial with a flowering stalk that grows up to 3 feet tall the second year. The flowers are about ½ inch across with a dull red color. Later they form a four-parted nut-like fruit which is covered with small, hooked bristles. A weed from Europe, it is found in waste places throughout the United States.

1/4x Van Bruggen photo

VENUS' SLIPPER

Calypso bulbosa Orchid Family June - July

This is an orchid which is one of a kind. There is only one species of **Calypso**, and it grows around the world in the north temperate regions of North America and Eurasia. Some readily admit it is the most beautiful of the orchids native to North America. The single flower is formed at the tip of a stem about 8 inches tall. Near the base of the stem there is a single broad leaf. In our area it grows in cool ravines of the Black Hills and eastern Wyoming.

1x Van Bruggen photo

WILD HONEYSUCKLE

Lonicera dioica Honeysuckle Family June

Flowers of the Wild Honeysuckle vary in color from red to yellow on the same plant. They are clustered at the ends of woody stems that trail or twine on other plants. Stems may be up to 6 feet long. Immediately below the flowers, two broad leaves are fused together to form a saucer-like base for the cluster. Lower leaves are ovate and have a white, waxy covering. Honeysuckle grows in rich and rocky woodlands throughout the western parts of Minnesota and Iowa, and west to the Black Hills.

3/4x Van Bruggen photo

CLUSTERED BROOMRAPE

Orobanche fasciculata Broomrape Family June - July

All broomrapes lack the green pigment, chlorophyll, which is necessary to make their own food. Consequently, they attach themselves to the roots of other plants, particularly sagebrush and wormwood (***Artemisia*** sp.). The clustered stems are 3 to 6 inches high with scale-like leaves that have no function and which wither and drop soon after they are formed. Flowers are creamy-white to off-purple, becoming brown towards maturity. The entire plant was used for food by Indians. Common in the high plains, this herbaceous perennial is intriguing to biologists because its method of reproduction is not well understood.

1/3x Stockert photo

SHOWY MILKWEED

Asclepias speciosa Milkweed Family June - July

This perennial is perhaps the most common milkweed of the plains. The herb growns in clumps from creeping roots to a height of at least 3 feet. The rose-pink flowers have specially long "hoods" and "horns." All milkweeds are highly specialized for insect pollination with the pollen massed into sharp, forked devices. These masses are removed when an insect's leg accidentally becomes lodged in the sharp angle. Small insects whose legs become trapped often die there because they cannot remove the pollen masses. Early settlers collected the downy seeds and used them for stuffing pillows and mattresses.

1x Stockert photo

BLUE VERBENA

Verbena hastata Vervain Family June - August

The erect stem of this slender verbena has several branches along the upper portion. Quarter-inch, lavender flowers form dense, narrow spikes that mature into seed pods. The lance-shaped leaves have sharply toothed margins. Growing up to 5 feet, this perennial prefers open, moist places throughout Canada and the United States. Some people believed that because the juice of this plant was ill-tasting it had to have some beneficial action. Consequently, it has long been used as a medicine. The verbenas, also called vervains, were considered sacred herbs in ancient Rome and were used in processions and ceremonies.

1/3x Van Bruggen photo

PURPLE PRAIRIECLOVER

Petalostemum purpureum Legume Family June - September

The small flowers of this perennial are only ¼ inch long and are red, usually not purple as the name suggests. The leaf segments are narrower than those of White Prairieclover (see page 64). The vegetative parts are fragrant when bruised or shredded. Prairie Indians prepared a tea by steeping the dried leaves of both this plant and White Prairieclover. They also chewed the inner portions of the deep, spreading roots. This herb produces a binding effect on bowels. It is a native throughout most of the Great Plains.

1x Van Bruggen photo

ROCKY MOUNTAIN BEE PLANT

Cleome serrulata Caper Family June - September

The young, tender shoots and leaves of this annual were eaten by western Indians. They also boiled the stems until a black residue remained. They used this as a paint or dye, or dried it to use later as food. The flowers have individual stems and several long stamens which extend up to an inch beyond the blossom. They attract a number of insects, including bees. The herb sometimes reaches a height of more than four feet and frequently grows in sandy soil throughout the plains states.

1/7x Stockert photo

RUSH SKELETON-PLANT

Lygodesmia juncea Aster Family June - October

Usually five white to pink florets make up each flower head. The nearly leafless, herbaceous stems branch from the base and grow to less than 2 feet tall. They appear as inconspicuous, greenish-gray skeletons when not in flower. A deep, spreading root system adapts this perennial to its dry prairie habitat. Several kinds of insects lay eggs in the stem which cause the formation of hazelnut-sized galls. Dakota and Nebraska Indians soaked the stems and used the infusion to bathe sore eyes. Indian mothers also drank the mixture to increase the flow of milk for nursing.

1x Van Bruggen photo

SULLIVANT MILKWEED

Asclepias sullivantii Milkweed Family late June - July

A showy perennial of low, moist prairies, this herb can be distinguished from most other milkweeds by its smooth, shiny leaves. Nevertheless, it is often confused with Common Milkweed (**A. syriaca**). Sullivant Milkweed, however, does not occur in weedy or disturbed places as does the other. The species pictured here with light lavender to purple flowers is sensitive to grazing and is a true prairie inhabitant. The fruits, called follicles, remain erect at maturity and contain many flat, silky seeds.

1/3x Van Bruggen photo

PALE PURPLE-CONEFLOWER

Echinacea angustifolia Aster Family late June - July

One of the prominent sentinels of prairie knolls in the northern plains, this herb transplants very successfully and makes an attractive border in gardens. The outer ray florets of the flower head are rose-purple and usually drooping. The dome-like center consists of disk florets and pointed bracts of equal length. These bracts remain for months after the seeds have been dispersed. Stems grow from 1 to 2 feet tall, bearing few lanceolate leaves. A hardy perennial, it has rough, blackened rootstocks that Prairie Indians used for medicine.

1/2x Van Bruggen photo

WOOLY VERBENA

Verbena stricta Vervain Family late June - September

The flowers of this herb are less than ½ inch across and are usually lavender, but may vary from white to deep purple. The blossoms form a long, fleshy spike, blooming from the bottom up. The stout stems cluster in groups and grow 2 to 4 feet tall. Coarse hairs cover the leaf and stem surfaces. Occurring in fields and prairies, this verbena's deep root system gives it the ability to resist drought. Native in the central United States and Canada, this perennial has spread eastward. Grazing animals avoid it because of its bitter juice. Vervain is another name for verbena.

1/3x Van Bruggen photo

WAVYLEAF THISTLE

Cirsium undulatum Aster Family late June - September

A native herb of the western plains, this thistle is often confused with Flodman Thistle (see page 90). However, Wavyleaf Thistle has a tendency to grow in patches and has thicker stems. The flower heads are also larger, commonly 2 to 2 ½ inches in diameter. Although both kinds overlap in their distribution, they are considered to be biologically distinct species. A true prairie inhabitant, Wavyleaf Thistle is a biennial and prefers well-drained sites. It ranges to the foothills of the Rocky Mountains.

1/2x Stockert photo

MARSH HEDGE-NETTLE

Stachys palustris Mint Family July

Typical of the Mint Family, the flowers of this perennial are highly specialized for pollination by insects. The blossoms have a two-lobed, upper lip and a longer, three-lobed, lower lip which serves as a convenient landing site for insects. ***Stachys***, meaning "spike," refers to the arrangement of the flowers on the stem. The hairly leaves shaped like those of the common nettle (***Urtica*** sp.) account for the name, but unlike the true nettle, the hairs do not sting. This wide-ranging herb grows in moist areas of the prairie and open places in alluvial woods.

1/2x Van Bruggen photo

BUTTERFLY MILKWEED

Asclepias tuberosa Milkweed Family July

One of the showiest of all moist prairie plants within the eastern part of the northern plains, this striking perennial provides a sharp contrast to green surroundings with its reddish-orange flowers. The lance-shaped leaves, 2 to 4 inches long, are softly hairy. Unlike other milkweeds, it does not have milky juice in its stems. Because of its color and odor, the herb attracts many insects, including butterflies. Indians collected the tuberous roots and cooked them for food or ate them raw when used as a medicine.

1/2x Stockert photo

SWAMP MILKWEED

Asclepias incarnata Milkweed Family July

There are at least 20 species of milkweeds that are widespread in the Great Plains. This is the only species of our region that is restricted to swampy or marshy places. A perennial, it has smooth stems about 3 feet tall and long, lance-shaped leaves. The flower clusters are rose to crimson red in color. After flowering, slender fruits are produced in pairs that are about 3 inches long and tapered at each end. Swamp Milkweed is more common in the eastern part of the northern plains.

2/3x Van Bruggen photo

MOUNTAIN THISTLE

Cirsium drummondii Aster Family July - August

The Black Hills of South Dakota are perhaps as far east as this thistle is found. It is native in meadows and valleys of mountainous regions in the northern and western parts of the United States and Canada. Usually rose or pink in color, the head is sometimes white. The stems are short, not more than 18 inches tall, but thick and watery. The long leaves, with many pinnate divisions that are spine pointed, make this a thistle easy to recognize in the field. Like a number of the prairie thistles, it is not a weed.

1/3x Van Bruggen photo

WOOD SAGE

Teucrium canadense Mint Family July - August

This mint has a flower structure unlike any other in the family. Typical of all the mints, the petals are fused and highly modified for insect pollination. However, the upper lip is only partly developed and reduced to small, horn-like projections on each side. The stamen filaments extend and arch over the large, lower lip that acts as a ''landing strip'' for insects. Wood Sage, also called Germander, grows in wood thickets throughout the northern plains. Plants are up to 3 feet tall with large, lance-shaped leaves. The flowers are arranged in a terminal spike.

3/4x Van Bruggen photo

WOOD LILY

Lilium philadelphicum Lily Family July

An inhabitant of woodlands and thickets from Maine to British Columbia, this perennial occurs in moist prairie areas of the high plains. The unbranched stems grow up to 2 feet from a white, scaly bulb that is edible. The narrow leaves are arranged in circles, or whorls, with 3 to 6 leaves in a whorl. There may be up to three reddish-orange flowers that are erect and very showy. Purple spots decorate the bases of the petals on the inside. This herb has western varieties that are deep red.

1/3x Kellogg photo

CANADA TICKCLOVER

Desmodium canadense Legume Family July - August

Tickclovers have segmented fruiting pods with tiny, hooked hairs that cling to clothing, fur and other soft material. Widespread in the East, a number of species range into the western plains, this one being perhaps the most common. This perennial inhabits moist areas, edges of thickets, and open woods. The herb grows erect, reaching a height of 4 or 5 feet with several flowering branches. The leaves are composed of three leaflets with the terminal one larger than the two lateral ones. The flowers, which darken toward maturity, develop into nutritious seeds which are eaten by upland birdlife.

1/2x Van Bruggen photo

SPOTTED CORALROOT

Corallorhiza maculata Orchid Family July - August

A perennial, this orchid lacks green tissues and is therefore a true saprophyte. It obtains its nutrition from the close association of its roots have with fungi called mycorhizae which live in the humus of the forest floor. The less-than-12-inch stems are fleshy with leaves reduced to scales. Flowers are brownish-white with purple spots. Though orchids are usually rare, this herb is frequently seen in rich woods from Newfoundland to the West Coast, including the Black Hills. Orchids should not be transplanted because most are rare and their natural habitat cannot be duplicated in cultivation.

2/3x Kravig photo

LONGTUBE TWINFLOWER

Linnaea borealis Honeysuckle Family July - August

This plant was named after the great Swedish botanist, Linnaeus. The small funnel-shaped flowers are slightly more than ½ inch long. Typical of most members of the Honeysuckle Family, the flowers are in pairs at the ends of slender, 3 to 6 inch stalks. These stalks and the nearly oval, evergreen leaves, about 1 inch long, grow from short, branched stems which rise from a larger, trailing stem. This woody-base herb inhabits woods and bogs in northern latitudes of the United States and in Canada. It is quite common in the Black Hills.

2x Kravig photo

THREE-NERVE FLEABANE

Erigeron subtrinervis Aster Family July - August

This herb is common in the Black Hills and in the Rocky Mountains, but is rare in western North Dakota. It inhabits open woodlands and other semi-shaded places. The stems, 1 to 2 feet tall, spout from a perennial, creeping, bulb-like root, or rhizome. The leaves have three prominent nerves extending into the blades from the leaf base; hence, its common name. Bright pink flower heads up to 2 inches across make it a showy plant when in bloom. Several closely related species are cultivated in the western United States.

1x Van Bruggen photo

FLODMAN THISTLE

Cirsium flodmani Aster Family July - August

A true member of the prairie, this thistle is usually found in poorly drained soils. After spreading by creeping rootstocks that are short-lived, the plant produces a stout taproot and grows about 2 feet high. The spine-pointed leaves are covered by dense, white woolly hairs. The flower heads are made up of tubular florets varying from rose to deep lavender. When in bloom, bumblebees are important insect visitors. Contrary to several thistles, this biennial herb is a native of the plains.

1x Van Bruggen photo

WOODLAND PINEDROPS

Pterospora andromedea Heath Family July - August

The unbranched stems of this perennial grow from the humus and underground parts of pines and other conifers. The herb lacks chlorophyll, hence it is called a saprophyte. Leaves are scale-like and not functional. The brownish-yellow flowers bloom along the upper part of the stem, each curved downward. After flowering, the fleshy stems remain as dried fibrous stalks for a year or more. Plants commonly reach 3 feet tall and in this area grow under pines in western South Dakota.

1x Van Bruggen photo

THICKSPIKE GAYFEATHER

Liatris pycnostachya Aster Family July - August

This tall gayfeather inhabits moist areas of the plains or roadside prairie remnants. Widespread in the eastern plains, it does occur westward in the eastern parts of the Dakotas and Nebraska. The stems are flexible and unbranched; many narrow leaves grow along the stem up to the flower heads. It is commonly over three feet tall when in flower. The heads are arranged in a dense spike, flowering in sequence from the top down. With some care, it can be successfully transplanted to gardens. Several horticultural forms similar to this perennial herb are cultivated as ornaments.

1x Van Bruggen photo

SWAMP SMARTWEED

Polygonum coccineum Buckwheat Family July - September

Many swamps and shallow ponds in the pothole region of the high plains may be covered with this herb which spreads by rhizomes, or bulb-like roots. Stems, which reach 2 to 3 feet high, inflate when growing in water. They bear oval leaves up to 6 inches long. Indians collected rhizomes of several kinds of smartweeds and ate them either raw or roasted. They have a nutty flavor and are nutritious. This perennial plant is valuable for retaining the vegetative cover for wildlife in marshy areas.

3/4x Van Bruggen photo

FIREWEED

Epilobium angustifolium Evening-primrose Family July - September

This tall perennial is one of the first invaders of disturbed soil. In a forest which has been cut through by a road or destroyed by fire, it will be seen for several summers thereafter. Mountain meadows are ablaze with color when Fireweed is blooming. Inhabiting high latitudes across North America, the herb is common in the Black Hills, though infrequent in eastern North Dakota. The rose-magenta flowers are inferior, meaning that the ovary is below the flowering parts. The ovary develops a slender pod, or capsule, containing many seeds, each with a tuft of hairs for easy dispersal.

1/2x Van Bruggen photo

HOARY ASTER

Machaeranthera canescens Aster Family July - October

White hairs covering the leaves and stems of this plant account for its common name. A biennial, usually less than a foot tall, it is a common herb of dry prairie, especially in the western part. The leaves are linear to lanceolate and are more numerous on the lower part of the stem. The color of the ¾-inch-wide flower heads varies around bluish-purple. When in bloom, the plant is particularly showy on dry clayish slopes.

1x Stockert photo

BUSH MORNING-GLORY

Ipomoea leptophylla Morning-glory Family late July - September

A frequent herb of dry prairie, Bush Morning-glory has several, many-leaved branches that grow up to 3 feet in height and 4 to 6 feet in width at the base. In the early morning hours during its blooming season, the bush may be covered with large, funnelform flowers. It grows from an unbelievably large taproot that may be over 18 inches in diameter at the top and up to 4 feet long! When under 5 years old, the root is not woody and is quite palatable; it served as a food source for the Plains Indians.

1/2x Stockert photo

COMMON BURDOCK

Arctium minus Aster Family August - September

A troublesome herb of overgrazed pastures and open, wooded draws, this biennial is more abundant in the eastern prairie. The first year it produces large leaves at the base of the stem; these leaves resemble those of rhubarb but are narrower and hairy. A single, stout flowering stalk appears the second year, growing up to 3 feet or more. The rose-purple flower heads have hook-tipped bracts which later dry and form a bur that catches on clothes or fur, consequently distributing the seeds. The Omaha Indians used the roots as a medicine for pleurisy.

1x Van Bruggen photo

SILKY ASTER

Aster sericeus Aster Family August - September

The oblong leaves of this perennial have long, silvery hair which press close to the surface, making it a striking plant even before flowering. The stems branch irregularly near the base and seldom grow higher than 18 inches. Each flower head is just over an inch across with 15 to 30 lavender rays and a yellow center. Silky Aster is typically an herb of rich prairie remnants in the eastern area of the Dakotas and is even more common in Nebraska and western Iowa.

1/2x Van Bruggen photo

SISKIYOU ASTER

Aster hesperius Aster Family August - September

This aster is frequently seen along stream banks and in open ravines at higher elevations. It ranges from Canada to Missouri, including the Black Hills where it grows up to 3 feet. The perennial herb spreads by creeping rhizomes, or bulb-like roots. Flowers vary from light pink to light blue. The principal leaves are lance-shaped, about 4 inches long. It transplants to gardens quite successfully, providing a showy display of flowers.

1/2x Van Bruggen photo

SPOTTED JOE-PYE-WEED

Eupatorium maculatum Aster Family August - September

The tapering leaves of this perennial are arranged in circles of 4 to 6 leaves with each circle at a various point on the stem. Its purple-spotted stems grow to 3 feet tall from a stout, fibrous root. Pink to purple flower clusters form a flat to rounded top that is very showy. The herb inhabits open, swampy places, often along streams. Native in moist places from Newfoundland to British Columbia, it ranges as far south as Nebraska. Although rare or lacking in western North Dakota, it is frequently seen elsewhere in the northern plains.

1/2x Van Bruggen photo

DOTTED GAYFEATHER

Liatris punctata Aster Family August - October

Found in dry or sandy prairie in the high plains, this herb produces pink to purple flower heads, each about ½ inch across, that form a dense spike. Each head has 6 to 9 florets. Several stiff, narrow stems grow up to 2 feet from a lemon-sized underground corm, a solid bulb-like root. Plains Indians ate the corms, but only as a survival food, for these perennial roots are coarse and fibrous, and not very nutritious.

2/3x Van Bruggen photo

ROCKY MOUNTAIN GAYFEATHER

Liatris ligulistylis Aster Family August - September

This perennial herb, also called Blazingstar, has purple flower heads that are larger than other gayfeather species. It also has long styles (the slender stalk of the central pistil) which project from the individual florets. Stems grow 4 feet tall from a hard, swollen base called a corm. There may be as many as 75 leaves on each plant. Very showy in moist prairie or damp soil along streams, it is native in all of the northern plains states. In the Black Hills it is particularly vivid in meadows.

2/3x Van Bruggen photo

WESTERN IRONWEED

Vernonia fasciculata Aster Family August - September

This perennial has tough, wiry stems which sprout in clusters from a heavy root system. These stems grow 2 to 6 feet tall, bearing narrow, sharply toothed leaves that are dotted by small pits on the undersides. Each flower head has 10 or more small, symmetrical, reddish-purple florets. These blossoms mature into hairy seeds which slowly turn dull brown before dropping. Preferring moist or low places in prairie or roadside ditches, this herb is rare in the western parts of the Dakotas and Nebraska.

2/3x Van Bruggen photo

ROUNDHEAD BUSHCLOVER

Lespedeza capitata Legume Family August - September

The creamy-white flowers of this open prairie perennial cluster into a dense head; however, they are nearly hidden by the bracts, or modified leaves associated with the flower. These bracts soon turn a rich brown, as shown here, making the flower heads very showy. Slender, flexible stems, crowded with many three-parted leaves, grow up to 3 feet. Dakota Indians cut the stems into small pieces and burned them close to the skin as a relief for rheumatism and neuralgia. Most bushclovers offer nutritious and palatable grazing for livestock and a food source of seeds for upland birds.

1x Van Bruggen photo

NEW ENGLAND ASTER

Aster novae-angliae Aster Family September

One of the most striking of all the asters, this perennial occurs from New England to the eastern part of the Great Plains. The stout stem commonly grows to 5 feet and branches at the top. Numerous hairy leaves clasp the stem. The ray florets vary from light rose to deep purple. This herb prefers a moist habitat, such as alluvial woods along streams. It is easily transplanted and does well as a garden border.

2/3x Van Bruggen photo

PRINCE'S PINE

Chimaphila umbellata Wintergreen Family July - August

This striking little perennial, shrub-like plant has shiny, evergreen leaves. They taste very refreshing when chewed and have been used as an ingredient in making root beer. The several stems may reach 6 inches tall in a spreading or ascending manner. Flowering stalks are about 3 inches long with an umbrella-like cluster of waxy flowers, each flower reflexed or curved downward. The outer parts of the flower are pink or rosy but the petals are usually a waxy-white, often tinged with pink. Each flower is about one-half inch across. Prince's Pine is found in sandy to rocky pine woods in the Black Hills.

1/4x Van Bruggen photo

ROUND-LEAVED WINTERGREEN

Pyrola asarifolia Wintergreen Family July - August

The rounded basal leaves, about 2 inches across, and a single flowering stalk or scape with rose-pink flowers are distinctive for this Wintergreen. Plants are perennial from a creeping rhizome system, allowing several to many stems to grow in a small area. The flowering stalks are about 6 inches tall, have 8 or more pink flowers, each more than one-half inch across. Later in the season a spherical fruit about the size of a pea develops, releasing many tiny seeds. This wintergreen is found in moist, rich woods in the Black Hills and across the northern United States.

1/3x Van Bruggen photo

PURPLE LOOSESTRIFE

Lythrum salicaria Loosestrife Family July - September

Until a few years ago, this plant was known only as an attractive garden ornamental. However, it has escaped cultivation, and because of its aggressive perennial nature and prolific seed production, it should be considered as a noxious weed. The stems may grow to 4 feet or more tall. The dense rhizome system, preferring moist or marshy areas, easily crowds out other plants and chokes ponds and streams. Flowers are red to lavender, each about one-half inch across. Each flower has 6 or more crinkly petals and usually 12 stamens. Literally thousands of fruits develop on the top 2 or more feet of each stem, with each fruit containing dozens of seeds. This weed is rapidly moving westward across the Great Plains.

1/6x Van Bruggen photo

NARROWLEAF PENSTEMON

Penstemon angustifolius Snapdragon Family May - June

The azure flowers of Narrowleaf Penstemon form at the top of usually curved stems. Occasionally several flowers on a plant may be pink or lighter than the usual blue. Most plants are not more than a foot tall, growing in clusters from a woody, perennial base. Leaves are 2 to 3 inches long, sessile (without stalks), and covered with a waxy surface. A native of the western plains, Indians used the roots of this herb for medicine.

2x Stockert photo

Blue Flowers

LANCELEAF BLUEBELLS

Mertensia lanceolata Borage Family mid April - June

This prairie herb has deep blue flowers that cluster on one side at the top of semi-arching stems that are 6 to 10 inches long. Each blossom is ½ inch long. The leaves and stems are smooth and white-waxy, without hairs. Leaves are lance-shaped, 2 to 4 inches long. The plant has a stout, perennial root which, if carefully removed, can be successfully transplanted to gardens. Although not abundant in any particular places, it is scattered throughout dry and sandy prairies in the northern plains.

1x Stockert photo

ROCKY MOUNTAIN IRIS

Iris missouriensis Iris Family May - June

Sometimes called Blue Flag, this meadow perennial ranges from western North Dakota south to Nebraska, and west to California. It is common in meadows of the Black Hills. The flowers are usually pale lavender but may be much darker or lighter. Stems grow up to 2 feet from a branched rhizome system. The rootstocks contain a bitter, resinous substance reported to be poisonous to livestock. Most likely the Plains Indians carefully avoided it. The herb can be easily transplanted to gardens.

1/7x Stockert photo

COMMON BLUE-EYED-GRASS

Sisyrinchium montanum Iris Family May - June

Except when blooming, this herb is very inconspicuous because of its grass-like leaves and narrow-winged stems. The six-parted flowers grow in small clusters from the stem. Each cluster is enveloped at its base by two bracts, or modified leaves, like the common garden iris. Three-celled, berry-shaped pods only ¼ inch wide develop after flowering, each containing several seeds. This perennial has fibrous roots and short rhizomes (thick underground stems) typical of the Iris Family. It is common in moist meadows in the temperate part of the United States.

3x Stockert photo

AMERICAN VETCH

Vicia americana Legume Family May - June

The common vetch of the prairies, this herb has eight or more small leaf segments of which the uppermost pair is modified into climbing tendrils. The stems are weak and straggling, occasionally reaching 3 feet long. They often climb more robust plants. The rose, or purple to blue, flowers are up to an inch long on short stalks. A valuable forage plant, Plains Indians also savored it. They prepared the tender, young stems and seeds a variety of ways. This perennial is a native of temperate North America and is common in thickets, moist meadows, and prairie grasslands.

1/2x Van Bruggen photo

PRAIRIE TURNIP

Psoralea esculenta Legume Family May - June

Called Tipsin by the Dakota Indians and Indian-turnip by early settlers, this perennial has roots which were an important food of plains inhabitants. In summer the 3 to 4 inch tuberous roots were peeled and stored so that they could be ground and pounded, providing a starchy meal. Plants are a foot high, much branched from the base, with flowers arranged in short, dense spikes. A small pod containing a pea-like seed forms later in the season. This herb is common on the northern plains.

1x Stockert photo

BLUE FLAX

Linum perenne Flax Family June - July

Blue Flax is a perennial herb that occurs in Europe and America. For years the American form was thought to be a different species. The stems are branched and about 10 inches tall. Its leaves are narrow. Because of the slender nature of the stems and leaves, it is largely unnoticed until it flowers. Then each branch ending is covered with broad, five-petalled flowers that make the plant very showy. Blue Flax is relatively common on hills and eroded banks over the northern plains.

1x Van Bruggen photo

RUSTY LUPINE

Lupinus pusillus Legume Family June - July

Of the many native lupines of the Great Plains, the Rocky Mountains, and on west, two are found in the western part of the northern plains and the Black Hills. This is the more common of the two. It is an annual, up to 10 inches tall with a single stem or occasionally branched. Leaves are palmately divided with 5 to 9 or more narrow segments. Blue to lavender flowers are produced in spikes at the ends of upper branches. As the flowers mature, the dense hairs on the stem and leaf petioles become rusty brown. It is found in meadows and open woods from the central Dakotas and Nebraska westward.

1/3x Van Bruggen photo

LONG-SPUR VIOLET

Viola adunca Violet Family June

As a group, the violets are notoriously difficult to distinguish with any degree of certainty. However, the Long-Spur Violet is an exception. A woodland violet, it has a short, above-ground stem with several heart-shaped leaves. At the base of each leaf stalk there are a pair of small bracts called stipules. These have prominent teeth at their ends. This characteristic, along with the unusually long spurs of the flowers, makes this violet easy to identify. In our area it grows from eastern North Dakota west to the Rocky Mountains.

1/2x Van Bruggen photo

LEADPLANT

Amorpha canescens Legume Family June - August

The leaden-gray leaves account for the common name. A very dense layer of short hairs covers the small, oval leaflets, masking the green color. The small, usually dark lavender flowers consist of a single, prominent petal and lack the keel (like the keel of a boat) and wings so typical of legume flowers. Leadplant, a deep-rooted, low shrub of the entire North American prairie is palatable and nutritious to livestock. Prairie Indians stripped the leaves to make a hot, tea-like drink.

1/2x Van Bruggen photo

SAWSEPAL PENSTEMON

Penstemon glaber Snapdragon Family June - July

The common name derives from the saw-toothed lobes of the sepals at the outer base of each flower. **Glaber** is from the same word root as ''glabrous,'' meaning ''smooth''; it refers to the waxy leaf surfaces. Stems of this herb are 1 to 2 feet high. Flowers are a rich blue and more than an inch long. A perennial of dry prairies, it is native from North Dakota to Nebraska in most of the high plains region except the eastern part.

1x Stockert photo

SLENDER PENSTEMON

Penstemon gracilis Snapdragon Family mid June - July

This later blooming penstemon has slender stems up to 18 inches tall. Each plant has 3 to 5 pairs of opposite leaves that are 2 to 4 inches long. The pale pink to light blue flowers are almost an inch long and are usually on short stems that grow from the axils of the upper leaves. After the petals drop in August and September, the maturing fruit capsules make the plant more conspicuous. Very common on dry and sandy prairie, this perennial herb is native from Canada to New Mexico and east to Wisconsin.

2x Stockert photo

ALPINE HEDYSARUM

Hedysarum alpinum Legume Family July

A number of wildflowers occur in the northern plains, especially at higher altitudes of the Black Hills, which are called boreal species. They are centrally native to regions which have colder climates—those closer to the Arctic Circle. At upper altitudes of the Black Hills this relatively inconspicuous plant may be found in rocky soil under pines. A perennial, the stem has a number of compound leaves, each with 11 to 21 or more ovate leaflets. The flower stalks are wand-like, with individual flowers arranged in a row on one side of the stalk. The petals are mostly lavender with occasional streaks of white.

3/4x Van Bruggen photo

SKULLCAP

Scutellaria galericulata Mint Family July

The Skullcaps are widely spread throughout North America as well as in the Old World. In the northern plains there are three species which are found in moist woods or thickets. The common name is derived from a translation of the Greek word **galerum**, which was a skull-cap worn by the Romans. This mint is a perennial, growing from creeping stems. The blue to lavender flowers grow singly in the axils of opposite leaves, giving the appearance that they are paired. The petal parts are about one inch long and fused together to give a structure highly specialized for insect pollination.

1x Van Bruggen photo

VENUS' LOOKING GLASS

Triodanis leptocarpa Bluebell Family July

The very narrow stems and leaves make this member of the bluebell family very obscure on the prairie. Flowers form along the upper part of the stem in the leaf axils. They are less than ½ inch across, usually blue or fading to lavender. The plants are annuals and grow from seed each year. The common name alludes to the shiny and polished appearance of the flat seeds that look like small mirrors. Venus' Looking Glass is one of two members of the **Triodanis** group that are found in the Great Plains.

3/4x Van Bruggen photo

COMMON CHICORY

Cichorium intybus Aster Family July

Originally a native of Europe, chicory is now a naturalized weed of roadsides and waste places in most of North America. It grows from a deep, perennial taproot. The stems are almost skeleton-like because of the irregular branching and the scarcity of leaves. A close look at the delicate flower heads reveals that each flower unit is a ray flower. In other words, there is no central disk of flowers as in many of the Composite group. The common name comes from the European use of the root as flavoring for coffee.

1x Van Bruggen photo

PURPLE VIRGIN'S BOWER

Clematis tenuiloba Buttercup Family July

Most of the virgin's bowers are climbing vines that grow up and trail over the lower limbs of trees in wooded areas. This one is of small stature and on occasion will climb but is usually matted or sprawled over rocks in wooded places in the Black Hills west to the Rocky Mountains. The leaves are three-parted and then sub-divided again. Deep purple flowers are solitary on stalks about 6 inches tall. The four, thin, strap-shaped, petal-like structures are actually colored sepals. A number of **Clematis** species are cultivated as perennials.

1/3x Van Bruggen photo

DRAGONHEAD

Dracocephalum parviflorum Mint Family July

An imported weed from Asia, Dragonhead is a biennial found throughout the United States. The stems are erect with few branches. Its leaves are lance-shaped and spine-tipped. Flowers are produced in a dense, almost head-like cluster with many spiny bracts. They are nearly obscured by the spine-tipped and toothed leaves. The shape of the flower suggested the Greek name **Dracocephalum**, which means "dragon-head." This plant does not have as strong an odor as found in many mints.

1x Van Bruggen photo

MONK'S HOOD

Aconitum columbianum Buttercup Family July - August

Wherever they occur, Monk's Hoods are relatively uncommon in terms of numbers. They usually grow in special habitats requiring certain soil types, along with specific amounts of moisture and shade. This one is found in the Black Hills and southwest to Colorado and the Rocky Mountains. The flower has a highly arched and purple colored sepal called the helmet. This results in a hollow crown. The opening of the flower is narrow and almost beak-like. Plants are 1 to 2 feet tall with several deeply divided "crowfeet-like" leaves. The plants, especially the seeds and underground parts, are very poisonous. The toxic alkaloid is called aconitine.

1/2x Van Bruggen photo

ARROW-LEAVED ASTER

Aster sagittifolius Aster Family July - August

To the not-so-careful observer, it may seem that the number of asters is very large. They are a difficult group to completely understand, but have enough individual differences so that identification is possible. There are over 20 species in the northern plains. This one is found in the eastern parts of the Dakotas and Nebraska and on south. The leaves are conspicuously arrow-shaped, which is the meaning of the word *sagittifolius*. The purple to blue flowers are produced in a loose spike on stems that may be 4 feet tall. It grows in dry and moist thickets or in woods.

1x Van Bruggen photo

BLUEBELL

Campanula rotundifolia Bluebell Family July - August

A number of common names are applied to this Bluebell, including Harebell and Bluebells-of-Scotland. It grows throughout North America as well as in the Old World. The bell-shaped flowers are distinctive of the family. Plants are perennial with clumps of stems that reach to 12 inches or more. The basal leaves are rounded, hence the term *rotundifolia*, but the upper stem leaves are narrow and linear. It grows on a variety of soils in both meadows and woods in the northern plains and in the Black Hills.

1x Van Bruggen photo

BLUE LETTUCE

Lactuca oblongifolia Aster Family late June - August

The blossoms of all the wild lettuces consist of ray florets, each with a single, strap-shaped petal. The flower heads of this one are very similar to Common Chicory (*Cichorium intybus*), a composite with blue blossoms in the eastern United States. *Lactuca* comes from the Greek word meaning "milk." It refers to the milky latex contained within the smooth, waxy stems of this perennial. Leaves are alternate and more narrowly lobed than other lettuces. Common on roadsides and in waste places, it may grow up to 4 feet. This herb is persistent and not particularly objectionable.

1x Van Bruggen photo

PALESPIKE LOBELIA

Lobelia spicata Bluebell Family July - August

This perennial, smaller than most other lobelias, has bluish-white flowers that are less than ½ inch long. The herb is slender, usually less than 18 inches high, with oblong leaves. It grows in moist, open areas but remains almost unnoticed among the prairie grasses because of its small flowers and stature. Sensitive of grazing and mowing, it quickly disappears if its prairie habitat is disturbed. Several varieties of this species are found throughout eastern North America.

2x Van Bruggen photo

TALL BELLFLOWER

Campanula americana Bellflower Family August

Tall, or American, Bellflower has bluish-lavender flowers that are shallow. Most other native bellflowers are more bell-shaped. The flowers each slightly exceed 1 inch in diameter and are borne along the stem in a spike-like, yet broadly curved fashion. Bellflowers are closely related to the sunflowers; the main difference between them is that sunflowers have many small flowers called florets in each flower head, whereas bellflowers do not have florets. These annual herbs grow in alluvial or most thickets in the eastern part of the plains where the prairies give way to the forests.

3/4x Van Bruggen photo

BIGBLUE LOBELIA

Lobelia siphilitica Bluebell Family August - September

The deep blue flowers of this herb, which are highly adapted for insect pollination, are arranged in a terminal spike upon a stout, unbranched stem. Leaves are in the shape of lance heads. The Indians used the leaves of closely related species for making tobacco. They probably used several species for medicinal purposes as well. Bigblue Lobelia was used for the treatment of syphilis and had little or no effectiveness. A variety of alkaloids have been isolated from most American species of lobelia, several closely related to nicotine. This perennial is common in moist, open areas along lakes and streams.

1x Van Bruggen photo

AROMATIC ASTER

Aster oblongifolius Aster Family late August - September

Occurring on dry, sunny slopes throughout the northern plains, this perennial is a good indicator of prairie that has had little or no domestic grazing or mowing. Short, oblong leaves grow from the stem which branches near the base, forming a wide, low outline. The flower heads are up to 1 inch in diameter; rays vary from pink to purple. The herb is easily cultivated in gardens, requiring no extra water.

1/2x Van Bruggen photo

DOWNY GENTIAN

Gentiana puberulenta Gentian Family early September

One of the really beautiful wildflowers of the true prairie, Downy Gentian, sometimes called Prairie Gentian, is perennial with erect, clustered stems that grow up to 2 feet. The deep bluish-purple flowers which are grouped at the top of the stem have plaits, or folds, between the corolla lobes. This herb ranges from the East Coast to eastern North and South Dakota. When it is found in the prairie, it is an indication that the area has had little grazing or disturbance of any kind.

1x Van Bruggen photo

PRAIRIE-SMOKE

Geum triflorum Rose Family May - July

This common spring wildflower of meadows and prairies all over the northern plains grows from a thick, perennial rhizome. The leaves are about 8 inches long, pinnately-parted with many segments, and grow from the crown at soil level. The flowering stalk or scape is about 12 inches tall, usually has three flowers, hence the species name. The visible outer parts, the sepals, are lavender to rose-colored. However, the inner petals are white but usually not very visible. Late in the summer each one-seeded fruit, called an achene, grows a long, plumose style, which remains for several weeks. These many plumes on each stalk wave in the wind which gave the common name Prairie-Smoke.

1/3x Van Bruggen photo

WILD BERGAMOT

Monarda fistulosa Mint Family June - August

Another common name of this widely occurring prairie plant is Horsemint. It is a relatively large perennial plant, up to 3 feet tall, and usually branched. The stem is square in cross section, like most mints, and the vegetative parts have the characteristic minty odor. Lavender to blue flowers are in dense, terminal clusters, each flower up to 1 inch long, with a tubular shape. The open end of the flower has an upper and lower lip, which is highly adapted for insect pollination. Native Americans used the leaves in boiled water for the vapor treatment of colds and other bronchial disorders. Wild Bergamot is found in prairies and open woodlands over the Plains.

1/5x Van Bruggen photo

NORTHERN FOG-FRUIT

Lippia lanceolata Vervain Family June - September

The tiny flowers of this marshland plant may vary from white to deep lavender. Because the dense spike of unopened flowers is purple-blue, it is included in this section. Individual flowers, only about one-fourth inch long, open for several months at the end of 1 to 3 inch stalks. Fog-fruit is a sprawling plant that roots at the leaf nodes, forming a large mat in wet places. The leaves are broadly lance-shaped, opposite on the stem, and dark green. It is frequent at stream margins, ponds and in prairie swales in our area.

2/3x Van Bruggen photo

FALSE DRAGONHEAD

Physostegia virginiana Mint Family July - August

False Dragonhead has showy, funnelform flowers over 1 inch long with a broad, 2-lipped throat. They flower over a several week period on an elongate, spike-like cluster. Plants are perennial from stolons or rhizomes, with stems up to 3 feet tall. The leaves are sharply serrate on their margins, lance-shaped, and about 3 inches long. It is common in a variety of moist places in the eastern part of the northern plains.

1/4x Van Bruggen photo

CLAMMYWEED

Polanisia dodecandra Caper Family July - September

The Clammyweed is closely related to the Rocky Mountain Bee plant, page 85. An annual plant with stems branched upward and with 3-parted leaves, it may be 6 inches to 2 feet tall, depending on available moisture. It possesses a rank, objectionable odor due to the clammy-like hairs that exude the fetid oils. The flowers are attractive with long, purple stamens and purple sepals. However, the petals are whitish to rose-colored. Later each flower develops a clammy-haired fruit not unlike a mustard pod which releases many seeds. Grazing animals carefully avoid this plant. It is frequently found in gravelly or sandy soils of prairies and floodplains.

1/2x Van Bruggen photo

SWAMP ASTER

Aster puniceus Aster Family August - September

This stately Aster with flowers ranging from light pink to deep blue may be 4 feet tall. It grows from a stout rhizome or woody root and has many ascending branches. The stem and lower leaf surfaces are covered with soft, white hairs. Its leaves are narrowly lance-shaped, their bases clasping the stem. Flower heads are over 1 inch across, with each ray flower nearly one-half inch long. The central or disk flowers are yellow, making an attractive color contrast. Swamp Aster is occasionally found in open, wet meadows in the northern plains but is rare in the Black Hills.

1/6x Van Bruggen photo

INDEX

BIBLIOGRAPHY

Fernald, M.L. — **Gray's Manual of Botany.** 8th ed. New York, N.Y.: American Book Company, 1950.

Gleason, H.A. and A. Cronquist — **Manual of Vascular Plants of Northeastern United States and Adjacent Canada.** Princeton, New Jersey: D. Van Nostrand Company, 1963.

Gleason, H.A. and A. Cronquist — **The Natural Geography of Plants.** New York, N.Y.: Columbia University Press, 1964.

Great Plains Flora Association — **Flora of the Great Plains.** T.M. Barkley, Editor. University of Kansas Press. 1986.

Harrington, H.D. — **Edible Native Plants of the Rocky Mountains.** Albuquerque, New Mexico: University of New Mexico Press, 1967.

Harrington, H.D. — **Manual of the Plants of Colorado.** Denver, Colorado: Sage Books, 1954.

Hauk, J.K. — **Badlands, Its Life and Landscape.** Interior, South Dakota: Badlands Natural History Association, 1969.

Kingsbury, J.M. — **Poisonous Plants of the United States and Canada.** Englewood Cliffs, New Jersey: Prentice-Hall, Inc., 1964.

Rickett, H.W. — **Wild Flowers of the United States, The Central Mountains and Plains.** New York, N.Y.: McGraw-Hill Book Company, 1973 (3 volumes).

Rickett, H.W. — **Wild Flowers of the United States, the Northeastern States.** New York, N.Y.: McGraw-Hill Book Company, 1966 (2 volumes).

Rydberg, P.A. — **Flora of the Prairies and Plains of Central North America.** New York, N.Y.: Hafner Publishing Company, 1932. (reprinted, 1965).

Straudinger, J.D. — **Wild Flowers of Theodore Roosevelt National Memorial Park.** Theodore Roosevelt Nature and History Association, 1967.

Stevens, O.A. — **Handbook of North Dakota Plants.** Fargo, North Dakota: North Dakota Institute for Regional Studies, Knight Printing Company, 1950.

Tomanek, G.W. — **Pasture and Range Plants.** Bartlesville, Oklahoma: Phillips Petroleum Company, 1963.

Van Bruggen, T. — **Vascular Plants of South Dakota.** Iowa State Press, Ames, Iowa, 1985.